Contents

Lionello Venturi

CÉZANNE

Preface by
Giulio Carlo Argan

SKIRA
M

First published in Great Britain in 1978 by
MACMILLAN LONDON LTD
London and Basingstoke

Associated companies in Delhi, Dublin,
Hong Kong, Johannesburg, Lagos, Melbourne,
New York, Singapore and Tokyo

ISBN 0 333 25317 5

PRINTED AND BOUND IN SWITZERLAND

Preface

WHEN I look back on my long friendship with Lionello Venturi, I cannot help feeling a twinge of remorse. Certainly I loved him like a father, but he loved me like a son, and that makes a difference. The affection that we his pupils felt for him was compounded of gratitude, admiration and respect; but these are sentiments anchored in the past, while what he gave us was sympathy, confidence and hope. With that optimism which was part and parcel of his character but which with him was also a moral principle, he saw in us the future of his ideas; and ideas do not repeat themselves, they evolve. He was pleased when he found in our work a train of thought born of his own ideas but differing from them. If, today, I were asked to describe Lionello Venturi in one word, I should describe him as a generous man—generous both in his humanity and open-mindedness and in his large and valuable corpus of writings as an art historian.

When in 1931 he left Turin University and Italy, having refused to take the oath of allegiance to the Fascist regime, he also refused to consider himself a victim. To those who called on him in Paris, in his beautiful house in the Rue Pierre Charron, he was wont to say that exile had in fact given him a timely opportunity for getting away from Italian provincialism and breathing the air of Europe. Likewise, when he returned to Italy from exile in 1944, he had no thought of seeking justice or vengeance; on the contrary, his one idea was to help Italy to regain an honourable place in European culture, from which Fascism had so long cut it off. He trained another generation of pupils, put the school in touch with the quickening forces of art, raised—and faced—many polemics, chiefly with those who, after the turmoil of Fascism and the war, longed for a quiet return to the culture of the past. Both his old and his new pupils were advised not to yield too readily to the authority of their masters, not even to his own; education, for him, was nothing unless pursued in freedom. And as he never departed from the luminist foundations of his culture and always saw criticism as providing the main framework of modern thought, he was impatient of criticism exercised in one sense only: he criticized us and expected us to criticize him.

The artists he chose to study numbered among those who have rebelled against the authority of the past and that of the academy: Leonardo da Vinci, Giorgione, Caravaggio. And Cézanne above all. It must not be forgotten that Lionello Venturi was the first scholar in Italy to admire the Impressionists and devote university courses to them, even though in the Fascist period the mere fact of showing an interest in French artists was considered an affront to Italian patriotism. Impressionism was a liberation from the oppressive authority of classicism and the academy; but with Cézanne began the elaboration of a new system of representation, differing radically from the classical system, since it regarded art as a total experience released from the constraint of any authority, whether theoretical or historical.

Some time elapsed between Lionello Venturi's earlier writings, which were modern interpretations of artists of the past, and the stage in his career when he devoted himself essentially to the historical interpretation of modern artists. In the interval, his writings dealt chiefly with questions of theory and the history of art criticism. These researches, which were only apparently marginal to the history of art, led him away from the aesthetic idealism of Croce and brought him closer to the German theorists of visibility: Fiedler, Riegl, Wölfflin. At the same time he studied the notion of "taste"; that is, the notion of the culture of artists, of their participation in the cultural system of their time, but also the notion of the renewal of that culture by their works and their experience as artists.

The history of criticism in turn permits us to go beyond the abstract concept of art peculiar to idealism and to grasp works of art in their temporal existence, in the significance which they assume for their own time and in particular for the artists themselves. Every great work, as Lionello Venturi gradually discovered, bears within it the criticism of an earlier culture and the foundations of a new one, so that it may appear at once as culturally mature and "primitive."

Having by then resolutely undertaken to single out and describe the processes of a specifically artistic culture—and consequently to make the transition from a criticism of pure reflection to creative criticism, to criticism which is itself an art—Lionello Venturi inevitably came to see in Cézanne the very embodiment of the modern artist. In 1936 he published the first catalogue raisonné of Cézanne's work: thus he concretely affirmed that historical research must embrace the artist's entire output or what might be called his pictorial biography. One of the recurring themes in Lionello Venturi's critical writings is the relation between the artist's daily life, with his inevitable and sometimes tumultuous participation in the historical reality of the period, and his existence as an artist as recorded in the history of his work—a history which may also be tumultuous. For it is certain that even as he worked on in the remote seclusion of Aix-en-Provence Cézanne shared intensely in the cultural issues and problems of his time; and it is precisely for this reason that his outer life ran on uneventfully, in apparent isolation, while his art, his painting, was the theatre of an intense dialectics and reveals a thirst for experience that was never satisfied.

It is no accident if this study of Cézanne, completed between the end of 1960 and the spring of 1961 (Lionello Venturi died on 15 August of that year), lacks a biographical chapter: for the biography of the artist is recorded in the sequence of his works and in the often chequered development of his researches. This book is divided into two parts of equal importance: a factual account of Cézanne criticism and an account of his development as a painter. The two chapters on the history of Cézanne criticism are revealing. Even before he joined the impressionist group, Cézanne was regarded as one of the great hopes of French painting. Taking over from Courbet, Daumier and Delacroix, he had established a solid basis for the further development of romantic painting in the direction of realism. It is therefore a mistake to see in his early work a phase of uncertainty or to interpret it as a failure of his creative impulse. When he began drawing nearer to the Impressionists—whose importance his critical acumen enabled him to grasp at once—he had already entered on the path that he was soon to follow up, fortified by his experience of Impressionism. A look at the history of Cézanne criticism thus puts an end to the legend which, especially after Zola turned against him, made so much of his difficulties of expression and his anguished need to work on in isolation at Aix; and one may wonder whether Zola's unexpected volte-face may not have influenced his deliberate choice of this way of life and work. What is certain is that the Impressionists themselves—even though, after their group exhibitions, they moved in different directions—knew that in Cézanne's studio something was brewing, that the most momentous art developments of a period already rich in innovations were there being prepared.

This book, then, can be said to offer a new image of Cézanne: his struggle against the institutionalized culture of the time and his elaboration of a new culture of colour-form; his primitivism, which was not a would-be ingenuousness but the clear consciousness of originating a new era of art; his obstinate determination to neutralize his life as a man in order to live wholly and unreservedly the life of his art. Lionello Venturi, unfortunately, never saw the very fine Cézanne essay by Merleau-Ponty in *Sens et Non-Sens* (1948), which remained practically unknown in Italy until 1962. There are some significant coincidences in their views of Cézanne; for example, the sense of an ever renewed and deepened life-experience in the service of a life-work, itself a renewal of artistic culture from the start; or again the awareness of an internal contrast, not "between sensation and thought as between chaos and order," but "between the spontaneous order of things perceived and the human order of ideas and sciences." These correspondences between the analysis of a philosopher, who was one of the most original thinkers of our century, and the insights of an art historian are proof enough that this book, published eighteen years after being written, is not simply the posthumous work of a great scholar but still has a vital contribution to make to the study of Cézanne.

G.C. ARGAN
Rome, March 1978.

Autumn, 1859–1860. (123^1/$_2$ x 41″)
Oil. Musée du Petit Palais, Paris.

Photograph of Paul Cézanne in 1861.

Cézanne and Contemporary Criticism

THE ART OF CÉZANNE was so new and original, so complex and revolutionary, and at the same time orderly and in a sense conservative, that in interpreting it I prefer to take the longer way round—to begin, that is, by tracing the reaction of contemporary criticism to his work, and his own reaction to that criticism. This is in fact an easier approach than it may seem, because Cézanne's personality as an artist was so strong that at every period of his life it aroused the greatest enthusiasm and the most violent opposition.

To go back for a moment to his youth, to the three inseparables at the Collège Bourbon in Aix-en-Provence, Cézanne, Baille and Zola, who from 1852 on went on long rambles together in the Aix countryside, in the Arc valley and as far as the Sainte-Victoire mountain, intoxicated with air and sun, above all with the high spirits of youth. It is significant that the poetry they loved and read and declaimed in the open country was first that of Victor Hugo, then that of Alfred de Musset whose "boyish jauntiness" and "bantering romanticism"[1] won them over completely. In other words, Musset cured the three young men of romantic rhetoric and set them to cultivating that irony which prepared the way for realism. So their literary and intellectual orientation around 1860 was a salutary one. Cézanne himself wrote verse that aroused Zola's admiration: "Yes, old chap, more of a poet than I am. My verse is perhaps purer than yours, but certainly yours is more poetic, more true; you write with the heart, I write with the mind."[2]

But Cézanne never took his own verse seriously; for him it was an outlet for his irony. On the other hand, though often a prey to uncertainty and fits of discouragement, he felt a deep and abiding passion for painting. He followed up the courses in French and Latin literature at the Collège Bourbon by reading the French romantics on his own. But if he wanted to paint he had to learn how, and so he enrolled at the Ecole des Beaux-Arts in Aix, where in 1858, at nineteen, he was awarded a second prize. He continued the academic study of art in Aix, then in Paris, when his father permitted him to go there as a student in 1861.

Not until 1865 did Cézanne arrive at a style of his own, academic teaching proving for him, as for so many others, the obstacle that had to be overcome. Zola, as a writer, was able to go on from the literature courses of a good French school to a prose of his own; the latter of course conveyed a new social and moral outlook which no one had expressed before, but the literary form in itself remained essentially traditional. In painting it was different. The pictorial form then and for long afterwards taught in art schools was a form drained of any traditional value or substance. Long before 1860 Delacroix and Daumier had decisively broken away from

Letter from Cézanne to Emile Zola dated 17 January 1859, with a symbolic pen drawing:
"La mort règne en ces lieux" (Death reigns in this place). Collection M. and Mme Leblond-Zola, Paris.

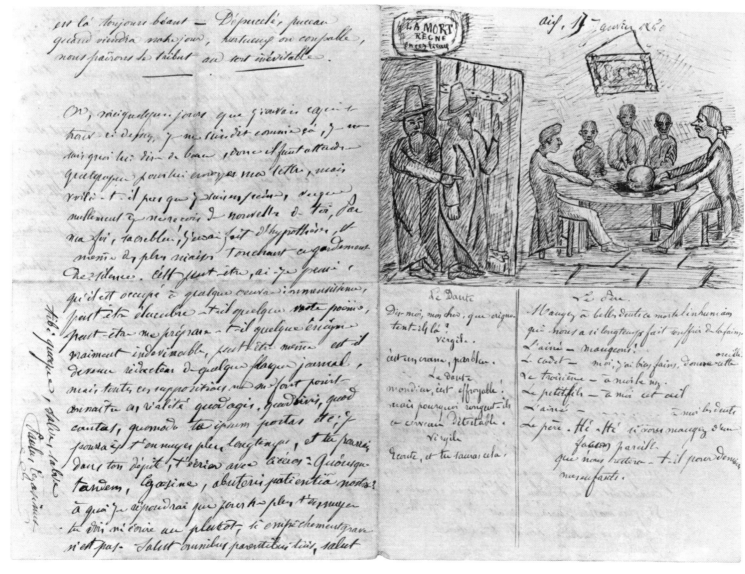

*Sketches and caricatures in a letter
from Cézanne to Emile Zola of July 1859.
Collection M. and Mme Leblond-Zola,
Paris.*

*Letter from Cézanne to Emile Zola dated
20 June 1859, with a pen drawing
of three boys bathing. Collection
M. and Mme Leblond-Zola, Paris.*

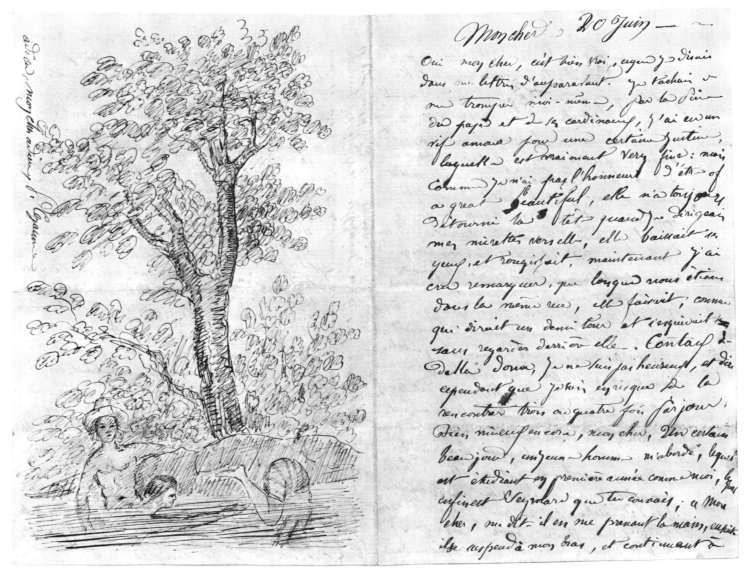

academic form. But the latter held its own in the schools, and outside them too; even Courbet had accepted it in part. While Cézanne was working out his own style, Manet created in *Olympia* an anti-academic form and set an example for the younger artists. Cézanne in later years was certainly influenced by Manet; but his early style, that of 1865, fails to show the impact of Manet, and indeed it appears at one stroke as being wholly his own, wholly original. As early as 1865, Marius Roux acknowledged that Cézanne, though "a great admirer of men like Ribera and Zurbaran, proceeds entirely from himself and gives his works a peculiar mark of their own."[3]

Memories of Delacroix and Daumier, as of Loubon, a mediocre painter active in Marseilles, had no effect on his work, except in points of detail. The originality of Cézanne in 1865 lay in a more radical break-up of academic design than any that had occurred in Europe since the academy had gained its ascendancy—that is, for some two centuries past. It was this break-up that aroused the enthusiasm of some and brought down upon him the fierce denunciation of others. When we remember that in 1865 Impressionism had not yet been heard of, did not yet exist, the rupture brought about by Cézanne can be seen as the prologue and beginning of the art of our century. From both the convulsive upheaval and the creative release to which it led, one can measure the tremendous effort made by Cézanne. Henri Matisse, who was conscious of the affinity of his own art with Cézanne's early style and reinterpreted his *Girl at the Piano (The Overture to Tannhäuser)*, realized that Cézanne's rich and tu-

Two Studies of the Male Nude, 1862. Pencil. (24 x 18^1/$_2$" and 23^5/$_8$ x 15^3/$_8$")
Musée Granet and Ecole des Beaux-Arts, Aix-en-Provence.

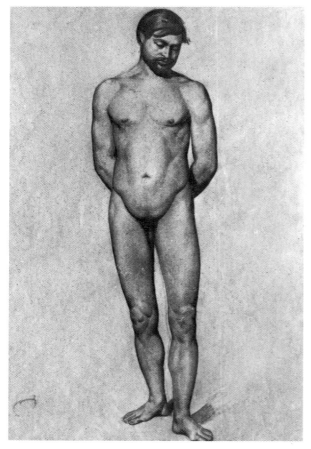 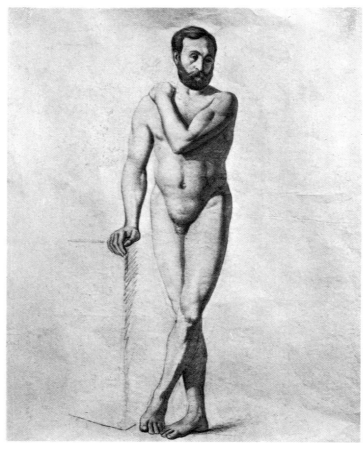

Still Life with Skull and Candlestick, 1865–1867. Oil. (18³/4 x 24⁵/8″) Private Collection.

Portrait of the Artist's Father, Louis-Auguste Cézanne, 1860–1863. Oil. (66 x 45") Reproduced by courtesy of the Trustees, National Gallery, London.

Portrait of the Artist's Father, Louis-Auguste Cézanne, 1868–1870. Oil. (78³/4 x 47¹/4") National Gallery of Art, Washington, D.C.

Eugène Delacroix (1798–1863). A Corner of the Artist's Studio, with Stove, c. 1830. Oil. (20 x 17¹/4") Louvre, Paris.

multuous sensations could only be reduced to order by a great effort of will—an unrelaxing, lifelong effort of will.

The academic teaching he had received led him by 1861 to admire Meissonier and Cabanel and conditioned all his work up to 1865; with the result that his forms remained clumsy because he felt them to be alien to him. But these early fumblings, as for example in the decorative panels of the *Four Seasons* which he facetiously signed "Ingres," have no connection with the style that made its appearance at

The Stove in the Artist's Studio, 1865–1868. Oil. (16¹/₂ x 11⁷/₈″) Private Collection, London.

one stroke in 1865. In this style there lingered something of the earlier gaucherie, which Cézanne retained with polemical intent. So that these pictures seemed monstrous in the eyes of the academic artists who made up the jury, the selection committee, of the Salons, and who systematically rejected these "monsters." Furthermore, all the rejected artists of the 1860s saw in Cézanne their leader, the most radical and intransigent revolutionary of them all.

In 1866 Cézanne made ready for the Salon some canvases "which will make the Institut roar with rage and despair."[4] He knew that they would be refused, and his friends prepared to support him with their own acclaim.[5] Of his own portrait as painted by Cézanne, Antony Valabrègue wrote: "A philistine of the jury cried out… that it was painted not only with the palette knife but with a spray-gun."[6]

All the realists were rejected that year, and on 19 April 1866 Cézanne wrote a letter to the Comte de Nieuwerkerke, Superintendent of Fine Arts, requesting that the Salon des Refusés should be re-established and describing his own attitude in terms of some arrogance: "I cannot accept the unwarranted judgment of colleagues whom I have not myself commissioned to appraise me… Let the Salon des Refusés be re-established. Even were I to be there alone, I ardently desire the public to know at least that I do not wish to be confused with those gentlemen of the Jury any more than they seem to wish to be confused with me."[7]

Both in Paris and Aix the circle of his admirers spread. In June 1866 Marion wrote to Morstatt: "Cézanne grows more and more. I really believe that his will be the highest and strongest spirit."[8] On 26 July 1866 Zola wrote to Numa Coste: "Cézanne is working; he is asserting himself more and more in the original path which his nature has impelled him to take. I hope for much from him." On

1. *Portrait of Antony Valabrègue, c. 1868. Oil. (45⅝ x 38½″) Collection of Mr. and Mrs. Paul Mellon, National Gallery of Art, Washington, D.C.*

2. *Portrait of Fortuné Marion, 1870–1871. Oil. (17 x 13″) Estate of Baron von Hirsch.*

3. *Armand Guillaumin (1841–1927). Self-Portrait, c. 1870–1875. Oil. (28¾ x 23⅝″) Louvre, Paris.*

4. *Portrait of Emile Zola, 1861–1862. Oil. (10¼ x 8¼″) Present whereabouts unknown.*

6 September 1867, after seeing the Manet and Courbet exhibitions in Paris, Marion wrote: "Really, Paul does much better than that."

So barely two years after Cézanne had initiated his personal style, he seemed to some the greatest of them all.

The preface to Emile Zola's *Mon Salon*, dated 20 May 1866, is in the form of a letter to Cézanne exalting their friendship of ten years' standing and their many discussions of art and life: "We have turned over tremendous heaps of ideas, we have examined and rejected all systems, and after such strenuous labour we told ourselves that outside of the powerful stream of individual life there is nothing but deceit and foolishness… Do you know that we were revolutionaries without realizing it? I have only just been able to say out loud what we kept saying under our breath for ten years."[9]

Even in Aix the public had begun to appreciate Cézanne. In October 1866 the painter Antoine Guillemet wrote from Aix to Zola: "He [i.e. Cézanne] is looking rather better, his hair is long, his face glows with health and his fine clothes create a sensation when he strolls down the Cours Mirabeau… His spirits, though always in a turmoil, clear up every now and then; and his painting, encouraged by some bona-fide commissions, promises to

21

Girl at the Piano (The Overture of Tannhäuser), 1869–1871. Oil. (22¹/₂ x 36¹/₄") Hermitage, Leningrad.

reward him for his efforts. In a word, the sky of the future seems at times less dark. On his return to Paris you will see some pictures which you will like very much… Their hue is golden and the look of them very fine… In a word, all's well, and in a short while we shall be seeing some very fine things, depend upon it."[10] And Marion wrote: "Paul has been for Aix like the germ of an epidemic, and all the painters here, even the glass-makers, are beginning to work with a thick impasto."[11]

1866, then, was a happy year for Cézanne, and Zola in a spell of despondency turned to him for cheer and comfort. It was a year not of success but of effort and struggle from which Cézanne seemed to draw fresh strength. His friends, however, were

disturbed by his occasional fits of discouragement in which he destroyed his canvases and slowed down the pace of his work.

In the autumn of 1868 Marion wrote: "Cézanne is working hard, with all his might, trying to impose order on his temperament, to force upon it the rules of a calm science. If he achieves his purpose, my dear fellow, we shall have some sound and complete works to admire."[12]

Trying to order his sensations, Cézanne painted some figure compositions and submitted two of them, *The Wine Grog* and *Intoxication*, to the 1867 Salon. They were not only rejected but pilloried in *Le Figaro*, so outrageously that Zola wrote a letter to the editor defending Cézanne.

From Aix, Marion wrote to Morstatt in 1867: "Paul is here doing some painting, more Paul than ever, but carrying with him this year a firm determination to succeed as fast as possible."[13] Marion added that, while no longer painted with the palette knife, his pictures were as vigorous as ever.

The figure composition *Girl at the Piano (The Overture of Tannhäuser)* seemed to Marion particularly successful. In Marseilles a Cézanne painting displayed in a dealer's shop-window attracted a crowd, some being struck by it, others manifesting their aversion for it.

Paul Alexis Reading to Zola, 1869–1870. Oil. (51¼ x 63″) Museu de Arte, São Paulo, Brazil.

Edouard Manet (1832–1883). Portrait of Emile Zola, 1868. Oil. (57¹/₂ x 45″) Galerie du Jeu de Paume, Louvre, Paris.

In Paris, Zola kept company with painters rather than literary men; he frequented the Café Guerbois where Manet was generally to be found in the evening, and where Cézanne rarely appeared. While Zola could appreciate Manet's powers as a painter of modern life,[14] his plastic insight was not acute enough for him to understand the art of his friend Cézanne; he saw that the latter had a vigorous and original talent, but the results seemed to him disappointing. While Marion was eager for Cézanne to exhibit his works, which showed, he said, "a really astonishing degree of skill,"[15] Zola did nothing to help his friend. Indeed, writing in 1870 to Théodore Duret who had asked him for Cézanne's address, he spoke his mind about him bluntly: "I cannot give you the address of the painter you ask me about. He secludes himself very much; he is groping for his way at the present time, and I think he is right in not wishing to allow anyone into his studio. Wait until he has found himself."[16]

Zola had manifestly lost his faith in Cézanne, and he never regained it. They remained friends, but Zola's aversion for his work increased. Indeed his failure to understand Cézanne was soon extended to include all the Impressionists, and even Manet himself, whom he had so warmly defended a few years before. The reason is perhaps to be sought in his immense success and popularity as a novelist, which may have prompted him to part company now with these painters who had failed to gain public recognition, and were not to gain it till many years later. In 1880, after dwelling on the hardships suffered by the Impressionists and their courage in facing them, Zola wrote: "The great misfortune is that not one artist of this group has powerfully and definitely achieved the new formula which each of them offers, scattered through their works."[17]

In saying this, Zola proved that his sensibilities were not fine enough for him to understand the art of the Impressionists, who by 1880 had painted their greatest works. But apart from the question of sensibility, it was a system of ideas that prevented Zola from understanding either Impressionism or Cézanne.

"Paul may have the genius of a great painter; he will never have genius enough to become one," wrote Zola tartly after Cézanne had destroyed a portrait sketch of him. Apart from the play on words, Zola here was reverting to what he had already said in a previous letter to Cézanne: "I have already told you so though: in the artist there are two men, the poet and the workman. One is born a poet, one becomes a workman. And you who have the spark within you, who possess what cannot be acquired, you complain when all you have to do to succeed is to ply your fingers and become a workman." Cézanne after 1860 *was* an accomplished workman; the two pencil studies at Aix (see page 16) prove it. But when he set out to make a work of art, it was necessary for him to go beyond craftsmanship, to achieve a synthesis between poetry and created form, not a mere addition of poetry and technique.

It was because he felt this more deeply and intensely than any other artist of the nineteenth century that Cézanne experienced an endless train of torments, misgivings and humiliations; and it is precisely for this reason that he was able to achieve an imperishable glory. Zola worked in a different way. When he had collected all the material he needed on a given subject, he wrote fast, pouring out page after page, never crossing out a word and, it is said, not even reading over his manuscript before sending it to the printer. It was a method on which he prided himself and one that impressed his public; but it is not a method that can give good artistic results. In 1872, when he was planning his novel *Le Ventre de Paris* (*"The Belly of Paris"*), a vast social fresco focused on Les Halles, the central market in Paris, he declared that he wished to produce "an immense still life," which he summed up as follows: "On the stalls, the fine fruit delicately arrayed in baskets had the well-rounded curves of cheeks that lie in hiding, of the faces of beautiful girl-children half glimpsed beneath a curtain of leaves; the pears above all, ruddy Montreuil pears, their skin as fine and clear as girls of the North, and the southern peaches, yellow and sunburnt, having the tan of the girls of Provence."

Look at a Cézanne still life and you will feel by contrast the bad taste of Zola, which arises chiefly from his desire to strike the reader by the objective precision of the description, and by choosing the most material and exciting objects which he presses upon us with a calculated skill that all too often fails to rise to the level of art. It is not inconceivable that to Zola, for all his assertive self-confidence and all the immense popularity of his novels, the thought of a bosom friend grappling with the difficulties of a new style came like a reproof for having fallen away from the ideals they had once shared, for having forgotten the pure aspirations of their youth and the art they had dreamt of together. This would explain Zola's revulsion of feeling against the friend he had once loved and admired. From that revulsion came, in 1886, a new novel in the Rougon-Macquart series entitled *L'Oeuvre ("His Masterpiece")*, the story of an unsuccessful painter partly modelled on Cézanne.

Zola sent him a copy of the book and Cézanne acknowledged it (4 April 1886): "I have just received *L'Oeuvre* which you were kind enough to send me. I thank the author of the Rougon-Macquart novels for this token of our common memories and I ask him to permit me to shake his hand as I think back on our early years." It was in effect a letter of farewell (as John Rewald aptly puts it),[18] full of nostalgia for the past, without any mention of the present; and from that time on he had no further relations with Zola.

What was the conclusion of Zola's novel? Its hero, the painter Claude Lantier—alias Cézanne—commits suicide because he realizes that he is a failure, incapable of attaining his artistic ideal. Thus did Zola pass judgment on the friend of his youth, writing without malice or hostility, intent on sincerity at any price; for his private opinion of Cézanne's work coincides exactly with that expressed in the novel. Given the literary usage of that day in France and the testimony of the writer Paul Alexis, who also, as early as 1882, was expecting to find himself misrepresented in *L'Oeuvre* and accepted it out of admiration for the art of his novelist friend, it is probable that Zola did not realize the mischief he was doing. Which goes to confirm that not only did Zola fail to understand Cézanne's art but even misjudged his character. The incomprehension of painting and sculpture revealed throughout *L'Oeuvre* is all the more flagrant because Zola had had every chance of being well informed and gaining true insights. The ideal of Claude Lantier is to paint "life as it passes through the streets, the life of the poor and the rich, in the marketplace, at the races, on the boulevards, in crowded back-alleys; and all trades shown in action; and all passions set up again, in broad daylight; and the peasants, and animals, and countryside!... Yes! The whole of modern life! Frescoes rising as high as the Panthéon! A terrific series of canvases that will make the Louvre burst!" But what has all this got to do with Cézanne's painting, with his aims and ideal?

In a draft sketch for *L'Oeuvre*, Zola wrote: "With Claude Lantier I want to depict the artist's struggle against nature, the effort of creation in the work of art, the effort of blood and tears to give one's flesh, to create life: always in combat with the true, and

The Temptation of St Anthony, 1869. Oil. (22¹/₂ x 30″) Stiftung Sammlung E.G. Bührle, Zürich.

Pencil study for "Afternoon in Naples (The Wine Grog)," 1870–1874.
Collection Lord Clark, London.

always beaten; wrestling with the angel... He is the incomplete genius, falling short of fulfilment: not much is lacking, his physiology is such that he comes a little within or goes a little beyond; and I add that he produces a few absolutely marvellous things, a Manet, a dramatized Cézanne, nearer to Cézanne."

The source of the misapprehension is clear. Whatever the poets of all ages may have thought, the artist's struggle against nature is something that has never existed; or rather it exists in the views they may express, in their words (also in those of Cézanne), but not in their art. Art and nature run on parallel lines and can never meet. To the end of his life Cézanne was tormented by his efforts to paint nature; but this torment must be distinguished from the paintings he actually achieved, which belong to the realm of art, not that of nature. Zola's tragic error, which goes back before him to Edmond Duranty, did not unfortunately end with Lantier's suicide in the novel, nor with the breach of a life-long friendship: it continued to spread in critical and public opinion, creating the legend of Cézanne as an artist of defective and unfulfilled powers.

Before 1870, it is true, there are some works by Cézanne which are notably unsuccessful: these are figure compositions on romantic subjects like the temptation of St Anthony, homicide, etc. Cézanne's form was ill-suited to give any literary value to a religious or historical theme. The subject got in his way and he failed to bridge the gap between form and representation; the quality of the colour and tone did not suffice to save the work. Before 1870 Cézanne had painted some wholly successful portraits, landscapes and still lifes, but no successful figure compositions.

It is interesting to note that something similar occurred with Degas. He accepted academic form as taught in the schools, but so far refined it as to turn it into a work of art. But not even Degas could

Edgar Degas (1834–1917). Medieval War Scene (The Misfortunes of the Town of Orléans), 1865. Oil. (33¹/2 x 577/8") Louvre, Paris.

Aeneas Meeting Dido in Carthage, 1873–1876. Pencil. (9 x 12") Henry Pearlman Estate, New York.

The Temptation of St Anthony (detail), 1869. Oil. Stiftung Sammlung E.G. Bührle, Zürich. ▶

succeed in history painting, of which *The Misfortunes of the Town of Orléans* is a characteristic example, and he had to turn to portraits, horses and dancers to achieve his early masterpieces. It would be difficult to imagine two men more unlike in their tastes and temperament than Cézanne and Degas, but both responded to the spirit of the time. Both were realists and as such limited themselves to certain subjects. They would have agreed with Courbet when he said that he could not paint angels because he had never seen any.

Cézanne of course had his own peculiar brand of realism. On 2 October 1866 Valabrègue wrote to Zola: "Every time he [Cézanne] paints one of his friends, he seems to be wreaking vengeance on him for some hidden offence."[19] With his southern temperament, he could not maintain the coolness necessary for seeing reality objectively. He felt the need for direct contact with nature in the open air and wrote to Zola in 1866: "None of the pictures painted indoors, in the studio, will ever equal the things painted out of doors... I see some superb things, and I must resolve to do nothing but open-air painting."[20] But for some years to come there was no trace of the open air in his pictures. Up to about 1872 the realism of Cézanne consisted in an impassioned introspection which went by the name of realism only because it was bodied forth with so much energy and no care for ideal beauty. It was expressionism before its time, more powerful than the expressionism that arose forty years later in Germany.

Then, under Manet's influence, this expressionism subsided, particularly in the still lifes, and gave rise to the lighter colouring that aroused so many hopes among his friends. And under Pissarro's influence from 1871 on he felt the need to paint from nature, not of course representing it objectively but interpreting it with the division of colours and the light effects initiated by Impressionism.

1

2

3

4

1. *Dessert on a Sideboard, 1873–1877. Oil. (23⁵/8 x 28³/4″)*
   Mrs. Charles R. Tyson Collection, Philadelphia Museum of Art.

2. *Edouard Manet (1832–1883). Portrait of Théodore Duret,*
   1868. Oil. (17 x 13³/4″) Musée du Petit Palais, Paris.

3. *Camille Pissarro (1830–1903). Penge Station,*
   Upper Norwood, 1871. Oil. (17¹/2 x 28¹/2″) Courtauld Institute
   Galleries, London.

4. *Thatched Houses at Auvers-sur-Oise, 1872–1873.*
   Oil. (18¹/8 x 15″) Present whereabouts unknown.

Bathers, c. 1890. Oil. (23⁵/8 x 32¹/4″) Galerie du Jeu de Paume, Louvre, Paris.

This change of style brought him some new friends. On 3 September 1872 Pissarro wrote to Guillemet: "Our Cézanne gives us some hopes and I have seen and have at home a painting of his of remarkable vigour and force. If, as I hope, he stays a while at Auvers where he is going to live, he will astonish many artists who have hastened to condemn him too soon."[21]

Though Zola, in the letter quoted above (page 25), had, incredibly, tried to keep him away from Cézanne, Théodore Duret had his eyes on him and wrote to Pissarro in 1874: "I would not mind seeing anything by Cézanne that you might have. In painting I'm on the look-out more than ever for five-footed sheep." Pissarro answered: "If you are looking for something out of the ordinary, Cézanne may be the man for you. He has some studies that are peculiar indeed, done in a way that no one else has attempted."[22]

The admiration of his fellow painters sustained Cézanne's confidence in his art. On 26 September 1874 he wrote from Paris to his mother: Pissarro "has a good opinion of me who have a very good opinion of myself. I am beginning to consider myself stronger than all those around me, and you know that the good opinion I have of my own abilities has only been reached after due consideration. I shall have to keep on working hard, but not in order to achieve the finish that arouses the admiration of fools. This finish which is so much appreciated by the vulgar is only a matter of handwork and renders any picture resulting from it inartistic and common. I must strive to make my things complete only for the pleasure of achieving greater truth and skill. And, believe me, a time always comes when one gains recognition, and then one has far more fervent and convinced admirers than those who are only attracted by empty appearances."[23] These words, with their confidence in his ultimate triumph, come

like a challenge to his detractors. Unfortunately he never repeated them. But they prove that, as an accepted member of the impressionist group, he had regained the ardour and confidence that he had already shown in 1866.

For artists at that time to understand the greatness of Cézanne, it was necessary for them first of all to repudiate preconceived notions about subject matter. This the Impressionists had done years before, and their point of view was set forth in 1877 by a friend and spokesman of theirs: "Treating a subject for its tones and not for the subject itself, this is what distinguishes the Impressionists from other painters... One knows in advance that with them one won't find either Joseph sold by his brothers... or Jacob wrestling with the angel, or Locusta trying out poisons, or Francesca da Rimini, or Mohammed, or Greeks, or Romans... but living scenes that sadden neither the eye nor the mind, luminous, joyous or grandiose landscapes."[24]

This being so, the Impressionists themselves could understand the art of Cézanne. "The artist most often attacked and most roughly handled by the press and the public for the last fifteen years is Monsieur Cézanne. There is no insulting epithet that has not been coupled with his name, and his works have only succeeded in causing laughter that continues as loud as ever... Cézanne is in his works a Greek of the great period; his canvases have the calmness and heroic serenity of ancient paintings and terracottas, and the ignorant who laugh at his *Bathers*, for example, put me in mind of barbarians criticizing the Parthenon. Cézanne is a painter and a great painter. People who have never held a brush or a pencil have said that he doesn't know how to draw and have rebuked him for 'flaws' which are only a refinement obtained by an immense skill... Cézanne's painting casts the inexpressible spell of Biblical and Greek antiquity; the move-

Portrait of Gustave Geffroy, 1895. Oil. (45³/4 x 35″) Louvre, Paris.

ments of the figures are simple and grand as in ancient sculpture, the landscapes have a compelling majesty, and his still lifes, so fine and accurate in the tonal relations, have something solemn in their truthfulness. In all his pictures, the artist moves us because he himself responds to nature with an intense emotion which his skill transmits to the canvas."[24]

Thus wrote Georges Rivière in the short-lived review *L'Impressionniste* published during the third group exhibition in 1877, chiefly organized by Renoir, whose views Rivière was probably echoing. These views, those of a painter who knew good work when he saw it, are in striking contrast with the poor judgment shown by Zola.

After the failure of the 1877 exhibition, the impressionist group began to break up and Cézanne never again exhibited with them. He was steadily rejected at the Salon, except in 1882 and 1889, through the efforts of Guillemet, but gained nothing by his two appearances there, and he may be said to have disappeared from the Parisian scene. The judgment passed on him by Zola and the Médan circle seemed to be confirmed, and it was emphatically endorsed by George Moore and Edmond Duranty.[25] Then, little by little, the current was reversed.

The Brussels group known as "Les XX" (The Twenty), headed by Octave Maus, invited him to exhibit with them in 1889, and Cézanne accepted: "Fearing criticism but too well justified, I had resolved to work on in silence, till the day when I should feel able to defend theoretically the result of my experiments."[26] He had always been interested in art theory; in 1865 Valabrègue wrote: "He sets forth theories and expounds doctrines."[27] And during the 1880s his theories corresponded closely to the change that came over his style, to that pictorial architecture in which his personality so perfectly expressed itself and which distinguishes him from the Impressionists.

The public, however, saw practically nothing of his work. A few of his pictures could be seen in the Paris shop of a poor but discerning colour merchant, the Père Tanguy, who showed them to younger artists like Maurice Denis, Emile Bernard and Paul Signac. First taken there by Gauguin and Pissarro in 1885, Signac at once bought a Cézanne from Tanguy.

The Impressionists were naturally the first to stand up for Cézanne against his detractors. Monet and Renoir repeatedly expressed their admiration for his work. Gauguin in a letter of 1881 begged Pissarro to reveal the mysterious "secrets" of the Aix master. Pissarro consistently defended him; in 1883 he chided Huysmans because in his book *L'Art Moderne* he had overlooked Cézanne, "one of the most astonishing and curious temperaments of our time and a man who has had a very great influence on modern art."[28]

Seeing how highly the Impressionists thought of him and noting the enthusiasm of the younger painters, several art writers were prompted to write about Cézanne, but they were bewildered by the novelty of his art.

In 1889 Huysmans tried to rectify his omission: "A revealing colourist who contributed more than Manet to the impressionist movement, an artist with diseased retinas who in the overwrought aperception of his eyesight discovered the foretokens of a new art—thus we may perhaps sum up this too much forgotten painter, Monsieur Cézanne."[29] Today it seems incredible that eye disease should be invoked to justify a new direction in painting.

In 1892 Georges Lecomte published *L'Art Impressionniste*, the first monograph on the movement. He felt obliged to acknowledge the greatness of Cézanne, but knowing neither the artist nor his works and so unable to devote a chapter to him as he did to the others, he merely referred to him as a member of the impressionist group. He admired the nobility of Cézanne and his exactness in the reproduction of objects. True (wrote Lecomte), he had in the past failed to observe proper proportions and equilibrium; but once he had returned to normality this marvellous intuitive artist had, with his fine luminosities and tonal accords, exerted great influence on his contemporaries.

In 1894 appeared the first serious and important study of Cézanne, by Gustave Geffroy,[30] and the artist thanked him for having "thrown light on what I have attempted to do in painting."[31] Geffroy too referred to the difficulty of getting to know Cézanne, "unknown and famous," a precursor of the symbolists, an example for Gauguin, Bernard and Van Gogh, a man with highly original endowments. "The history of art is made up of a network of main roads and branch lines, and Cézanne has at the very least dominated one of these latter... Cézanne does not approach nature with an artistic programme... not that he has no programme, no law, no ideal, but they do not come to him from art, they come from the ardour of his curiosity, from his desire to possess the things that one sees and that he admires... Even were one unaware of that, the works of Cézanne would convey it plainly and tell of the straining towards reality, of patience, long exertion, artistic integrity and a scrupulousness not easily satisfied. It is quite obvious that the painter is frequently incomplete... Whatever the subject he has tackled, there is true sincerity in Cézanne, the sometimes charming, sometimes painful mark of a will which satisfies itself or fails... Surely this man has experienced and is experiencing a fine inward romance, and the demon of art lives within him."[30]

For the first time an art critic had understood the "primitive" source of Cézanne's art and his

L'Estaque, 1878–1879. Oil. (23½ x 28¾″)
Galerie du Jeu de Paume, Louvre, Paris.

Portrait of Ambroise Vollard, 1899. Oil.
(39 3/8 x 31 7/8") Musée du Petit Palais, Paris.

Four Women Bathers, pencil drawing of 1879–1882 reproduced
on the cover of the catalogue of the Cézanne exhibition,
May-June 1898, Galerie Vollard, Paris. Fondation Doucet, Paris.

Maurice Denis (1870–1943). Homage to Cézanne, 1900. Oil. (71 x 94 1/2") Musée National d'Art Moderne, Paris. From left to right: Odilon Redon, Edouard Vuillard, André Mellerio, Ambroise Vollard, Maurice Denis, Paul Sérusier, Paul Ranson, Ker-Xavier Roussel, Pierre Bonnard, and Madame Denis.

commanding position with the younger men. The limitations of Geffroy were those of his time, of the prevailing realism, so that he could only see the artist's style in terms of his interpretation of nature.

Gustave Caillebotte died in 1894 leaving to the Musée du Luxembourg his collection of impressionist paintings, including two by Cézanne. The controversy over the Caillebotte bequest lasted until 1896 and helped to make Cézanne's name better known. So it was that Ambroise Vollard, who in 1892 had seen some of his pictures in Père Tanguy's shop, courageously undertook to hold a Cézanne exhibition in his gallery. It opened in November 1895, and Cézanne's fame dates from that show.

Discerning collectors, both French and foreign, came forward and bought his pictures: the Comte Isaac de Camondo, Auguste Pellerin, Charles Loeser, Egisto Fabbri. On 28 May 1899 Fabbri wrote to Cézanne: "I have the good fortune to possess sixteen of your works. I know their austere and aristocratic beauty—they are for me the noblest thing in modern art. And often in looking at them, I have wished I could tell you by word of mouth the emotion that I experience." Cézanne's reply is typical of him: "The number of studies of mine to which you have given hospitality assures me of the great sympathy for art of which you kindly give me proof... The fear of seeming inferior to what is expected of a person presumed to be capable of rising to any occasion may doubtless excuse the obligation I feel to live in seclusion."[32]

Before 1900, with a few exceptions, Cézanne was suspicious of people who sprang to the defence of his art. His very sensitive feelings, combined with a very strong *amour-propre*, created in him a touchiness that legend amplified out of all proportion. It made him a prey to outbursts of fury that subsided as quickly as they arose, but facilitated neither his life nor his art. On the other hand, his single-minded pursuit of perfection, his sense of his own dignity, his discreet acceptance of the ways or failings of others, gave him a humility which was a source of strength, but also led to a voluntary mortification which was both detrimental and dangerous. On 30 April 1896 he wrote to Joachim Gasquet: "Do you not see what a sad plight I am reduced to? Not master of myself, a man who does not exist... But I curse the X's and a rascal or two who, to write a fifty-franc article, have drawn attention to me... True, an artist desires to rise intellectually as much as possible, but the man should remain obscure. The pleasure for him should lie in study... You expect me at my age to still believe in something? More-over I am like a dead man." And he quoted the lines by Alfred de Vigny:

Seigneur, vous m'aviez fait puissant et solitaire,
Laissez-moi m'endormir du sommeil de la terre.[33]

It is distressing to find that, at the very moment of triumph, this formidable fighter whom nothing had been able to deflect from his purpose, neither the indignation of the public nor the falling away of friends, looked upon himself as one dead to the world.

All this time his reputation and fame were growing. A few of his paintings were shown at the Salon des Indépendants in 1901 and 1902. Three were exhibited at the Paris World's Fair in 1900. A one-man show held in conjunction with the Salon d'Automne in 1904 excited great interest; it was followed by two more at the same Salon in 1905 and 1906, each including ten works. In 1901 Maurice Denis exhibited his *Homage to Cézanne*. In 1905 the literary review *Mercure de France*, in the course of a "survey on present tendencies in art," asked the question: "What do you think of Cézanne?" Most of the painters questioned replied with respect, some with enthusiasm. Many of the younger men made the pilgrimage to Aix to see the prophet of the new art: the painters Maurice Denis, K.X. Roussel, Emile Bernard, Charles Camoin, J.F. Schnerb, R.P. Rivière, Gaston Bernheim de Villers, and the writers Edmond Jaloux, Joachim Gasquet, Léo Larguier, Joseph d'Arbaud, Emmanuel Signoret, Louis Aurenche, Marc Lafargue, Jules Borély and Jean Royère.

By 1900 Cézanne came to realize that the interest he had aroused was not a speculation made by journalists but a conviction held by artists, and to this he responded. When in 1902 Maurice Denis begged him to exhibit his work, Cézanne wrote to Vollard: "It seems to me that I cannot hold aloof from young people who have conducted themselves towards me in so sympathetic a manner. If I do exhibit, I do not think this will give a false idea of the progress of my studies." In 1904, when he exhibited thirty-three paintings at the Salon d'Automne in a room specially set aside for them, he revisited Paris and was pleased at his success. But he was too old to keep up the struggle and after a few weeks in Paris he withdrew to the Forest of Fontainebleau and then returned to Aix for good.

On 15 October 1906 he wrote: "I think the younger painters much more intelligent than the others. The old ones cannot see in me anything but a disastrous rival... A little moral satisfaction, but work alone can give me that, would do much for me." Those words are a spiritual testament: resigned to not being understood, he expressed his faith in youth; desiring some moral satisfaction, he did not look for it in the judgment of others but expected it only from his work.

Between 1895 and Cézanne's death in 1906, his art gained an ever wider circle of admirers. Even the public, so long bewildered by his art, seemed less hostile. And since that hostility sprang from the very novelty of his work, which went deeper than that of his impressionist friends, the time had come for the critics to explain and justify what had seemed incomprehensible to the public.

The first attempts to define his art betray a note of perplexity. Reviewing the 1895 exhibition at Vollard's, Gustave Geffroy wrote: "Cézanne is on the one hand a traditional artist, steeped in those whom he regards as his masters, and on the other an observer as scrupulous as a primitive intent on accuracy. He knows art and he wants to force it to reveal itself directly through things. He is neither ignorant nor shrewd: there, by elimination, is a definition of him as an artist... Ardent and ingenuous, harsh and discriminating, he is a great stickler for the truth. He will be in the Louvre."[34]

Also writing in 1895, pointing out that even those most favourable to Cézanne sought to justify their admiration by describing him as an incomplete artist, Thadée Natanson protested: "*Complete*, an epithet hypocritically synonymous with profitable for eager dealers and greedy speculators intent on getting the most for their money... No less inexpressible is that grace and delicacy which the artist diffuses everywhere and which finds its crowning touch in the pure tonal relations that at first seemed coarse, only because they are so rare. This forthrightness which the misguided might be tempted to describe as brutal—how it contrives to make most of these images pretty, in the best sense of the word... A certain heedlessness unconcerned with what is not its main object, and disdaining to please, proclaims a master." For Natanson, Cézanne was more than a precursor: "Already he takes his place in French painting as the new master of still life."[35] As there was no longer any hierarchy of subjects, this means he had attained one kind of perfection.

A similar view was expressed in 1904 by Roger Marx, writing about the still lifes: "Here the colourist's gifts attain so intense a pitch of expression that painting seems never to have better shown the power of human genius to impart life."

The 1895 exhibition at Vollard's aroused a certain sympathy for Cézanne, even in writers like Camille Mauclair and André Fontainas who soon relapsed into hostility. André Mellerio saw him as a precursor of the "idealist" (i.e. symbolist) movement: "In Cézanne there is something at once naïve and refined. Of nature he gives a version all his own in which the juxtaposition of hues and the arrangement of lines make his so forthright painting a kind of synthesis of colours and forms in their intrinsic beauty. It is as if he wished to restore to each object its original form, intact, not devitalized by art practices, its true and essential lustre."[36]

Seated Woman Bather, 1873–1877. Pencil.
(7⁷/₈ x 11¹³/₁₆″) Present whereabouts unknown.

Seated Woman Bather, 1873–1877. Oil.
Present whereabouts unknown.

With Mellerio, Cézanne criticism made a step forward, for he was the first to point out the idealist character of this painting. This may be identified with the synthesis already noted by Van Gogh in 1889: "For, yes, you must feel the whole of a country—isn't that what distinguishes a Cézanne from anything else?"[37] But for Mellerio this synthesis lay also in the intrinsic beauty of the colours and forms, which represented a departure from the naturalistic conception of art.

The "primitive" character of Cézanne's art was stressed by Félicien Fagus in 1899: "Before nature he is like a child, one feels; he no longer feels, he no longer cares about, anything but his craft; he sees and transposes what he sees, with all the overwrought responses of his eye and all the resources accumulated in his hand. So that his works take on the brutal, impulsive charm of something childish: that naïveté, that innocence, the supreme effect of skill in perpetual worship of nature."[38]

Of particular importance is the essay written by Emile Bernard after a visit to Aix in 1904.[39] At that time, not yet wedded to a theory of his own, he was receptive to Cézanne's views, making no attempt to force them into the mould of his own idealist attitude, as he did in his book of 1921. Bernard moreover, as a symbolist close to Gauguin, could understand Cézanne's principles better than other painters; and his 1904 account of Cézanne's views on art is not only plausible but confirmed by Cézanne's own letters.

Cézanne had broken with Impressionism: that is the first point that Bernard makes, maintaining that by now (that is, in 1904) Cézanne alone *remained*, Monet for all his merits having been surpassed. Cézanne's kinship was with Delacroix, "an artist of imaginative and sensitive insight into colour, the rarest and most powerful of gifts." And what, precisely, Cézanne had done was to express

Maurice Denis (1870–1943).
A Visit to Cézanne at Aix, 1906. Oil.
(20 x 25¹/₄″) Private Collection.

Two photographs of Cézanne painting at Aix, taken by Emile Bernard about 1905.

his sensations of colour; these depend of course on the eye but their full development depends on the brain. After receiving the tutelage of Pissarro at Auvers, Cézanne had arrived at that "astounding creation of a sincere and so naïvely skilful art which he has since shown us." The elements of this art were "the raising of form towards a decorative conception and of colour towards the most musical pitch. So that as the artist works on, the further he gets from objectivity, from the opacity of the model he started from, and the deeper he goes into sheer painting for its own sake; the more he abstracts his picture, the more broadly he simplifies it, after a narrow, conforming, hesitant commencement." Cézanne's slow and fervid elaboration of each work shows that his analysis is the means by which he creates a synthesis, a demolition and reconstruction tantamount to a *supernature.*

No one before Bernard had pointed out the abstract character of a Cézanne painting. Instead of taxing it with incompleteness, he considers the result for its own sake, as something apart from nature, as pure painting. "Far from being spontaneous, Cézanne is a man who thinks, his genius is a flash of lightning in depth. As a result, his temperament has led him to new creations, to unexpected syntheses." His works "constitute the finest attempt at a renewal of painting and colour that France has seen since Delacroix."[39] Bernard was patently unfair to the Impressionists and there is some confusion in his notion of decoration, which for him meant both breaking away from the model and reducing a representation in depth to a surface pattern—two essentially different notions. Nor can Cézanne's style be equated with mysticism and musicality, as Bernard would have it. He is happier when he defines its beauty as "the absolute expression of the art employed"—as, in other words, the perfection of art.

In 1905 Charles Morice, the friend and biographer of Gauguin, held in the *Mercure de France* his inquiry into the tendencies of contemporary art.[40] Was Impressionism finished? Had Gauguin and others introduced any new elements? What about Cézanne? How independent of nature should art be? Paterne Berrichon replied that Cézanne was "an incomparable treasure of luminous emotion," as important in painting as Rimbaud in literature. For Gaston Prunier he was a personality impervious to influence who had compelled acceptance of his own ideal. For Charles Camoin he was a genius by virtue of the novelty and scope of his achievement. He was one of those who shape the course of art. "He has only sought to *vivify Poussin from nature.*" Albert Brant replied: "I consider Cézanne as one of the greatest masters of French art and I have the sincerest admiration for his work." Antoine de La Rochefoucauld, though disliking Impressionism, admired Cézanne: "A painter of genius. I love the integrity and strength of his work, unamenable to any convention... No one more than he has possessed naïveté combined with power... Personally I prefer his portraits, his male and female bathers and his figure compositions." Here is a point of view worth noting, a critic who perceived something else besides the naturalistic perfection of the still lifes, which others, like Bernard Boutet de Monvel, especially admired.

Paul Sérusier, the follower of Gauguin (to whom he owed the revelation of Cézanne's art), wrote that he "has shown clearly that the imitation of nature is only a means, that the sole aim is to dispose the lines and colours on a given surface so as to charm the eyes, to speak to the mind, to create by purely pictorial means a language or rather to regain the universal language... If, as I venture to hope, a tradition is to spring from our time, it is from Cézanne that it will spring." This is a significant testimony: the younger men schooled by Gauguin looked back to Cézanne as the master who had shown the way to artistic creation over and above nature imitation.

Naturally praise was tempered with qualifications. Emile Schuffenecker, Gauguin's friend, wrote: "Great and harsh in his ingenuousness, Cézanne is a temperament. He has failed to produce either a picture or an oeuvre." Common at that time was this expectation that a painter should produce a large body of work and compositions with many figures. It was this academic view, already expressed by Zola, that Impressionism and Cézanne demolished, as the subsequent course of art was to show.

Others objected to his "gaucherie," his "heavy" form, his "hunch-backed" nudes, his lack of finish. For René X. Prinet, his "admirably gifted" eye and temperament were "in the service of an unskilled hand. An instinctive synthesis alone guides that hand. If he appeals to so many young people, it is because they choose to see only his gifts; the older painters are too proud of their skill to like and understand him." This is a shrewd judgement, singling out the part played by Cézanne in liberating the artist's intuition from subservience to manual skill.

The *Mercure de France* also reported the antipathy to Cézanne expressed by various writers and artists in commonplace terms. The 1905 survey of opinion[40] is important as showing that a year before Cézanne's death the greatness of his art had been understood, if only by a limited circle of admirers, and some of its essential characteristics defined: its powerful originality with respect to Impressionism and indeed all French painting; the primitive, ingenuous side of his temperament that made him rebel against convention and manual skill and commit himself to spontaneous creation; the absolute value of his style with respect to naturalism, as that style appears in the scenes of bathers, as the creation of a pictorial language from which a new tradition would spring.

The younger artists could respond to Cézanne's gift of spontaneous creation, but the older men were too much attached to their conventions. He was no longer, then, the precursor who had failed to realize form, no longer the incomplete genius, but the master who had initiated a new tradition. In October 1907, one year after his death, an important retrospective was held at the Salon d'Automne. Both his admirers and detractors were confirmed in their opinion by this large showing of fifty-six oils and watercolours. Charles Morice was more enthusiastic than ever.

In 1906 Théodore Duret published the second edition of his book *Les Peintres Impressionnistes*: he emphasized the Provençal character of Cézanne's art, his limited subject matter and the *pure* value of his painting.

In 1907 Maurice Denis published an essay[41] which falls into two parts: first, a very shrewd and understanding analysis of Cézanne's qualities as a painter; then his own theory of classicism, arbitrarily applied to Cézanne. In front of one of his pictures "we think only of painting; neither the object represented nor the subjectivity of the artist holds our attention." Cézanne, he felt, is opposed to Impressionism because, in giving primacy to sense responses, the Impressionists destroyed not only the lifeless conventions of the schools but also the necessary methods that went with them; Cézanne, on the other hand, "respected the essential role of the sense responses while substituting reflection for empiricism." Thus had the old masters done, and like them Cézanne attached great importance to composition, applying himself at the same time to the representation of the *motif*—that is, the initial vision of nature. For the subject he substituted the motif, so that his art is closer to a Persian carpet than to a scene by Delacroix. "Instead of evoking his mood by means of the subject represented, it is for the work itself to convey the initial sensation." Whatever Denis may have thought, this is symbolism, not classicism.

In 1908 the Italian critic Ardengo Soffici published an essay[42] praising the stylistic achievement and spiritual unity of Cézanne's art in which external truth is subordinated to internal truth.

The first German appreciation was that of Julius Meier-Graefe in *Cézanne und seine Ahnen*, 1910, an initial attempt to place him within the historical development of painting. While Meier-Graefe's historical synthesis seemed scholarly at the time, today it appears weak on the artistic side. He did however note the aristocratic character of Cézanne's art, as opposed not only to the artist's own character but to French painting after David and to Impressionism in particular.

In 1910 Jacques Rivière had some penetrating comments to make.[43] "Cézanne was not the sublime blunderer that a certain legend would have us imagine. His watercolours reveal on the contrary a staggering skill... When painting in oils, his hand quivers with the same skill, but he contains it. He is on his guard: he stands in fear of substituting himself for his sincerity... the line would leap... But Cézanne compels it to remain *eager*... In a Cézanne landscape one notices first its verticality: the picture's weight bears downwards... he had the love of *place*; he understood how fervently objects adhere to the place that is given to them... No less than by their *situation*, I am moved by the *duration* of these canvases. The same weight that maintains things in space maintains them in time... The colour... is not the colour that light sprinkles and spreads like water over objects... it is motionless, it comes from the depth of the object, from its essence; it is not its envelope, but the *expression* of its inner make-up."

For him, Cézanne the man was hidden behind his work.

In 1914 the Bernheim-Jeune gallery published a handsome, illustrated book on Cézanne.[44] In his preface Octave Mirbeau extolled him as "the most painterly of all painters, a painter who never cluttered his work with concerns foreign to painting." Léon Werth, in his critical essay, acknowledged the difficulty of understanding Cézanne due to the antinomies of his art. His is pure painting, abstract as a colour pattern, yet scrupulously representing a piece of reality which in fact Cézanne disliked. "One can thus understand why it is that some of his canvases, from their outward appearance, often bring to mind the paintings in a fair booth and that others are imbued with so tragic and so absolute a gravity. They seem shrouded in the silence of the museums. And standing in front of them, one is moved as if entering a cathedral. One's voice is hushed."

In 1914, too, the dealer Ambroise Vollard published his large book on Cézanne,[45] valuable for his personal knowledge of the artist, but without any critical pretensions. Then came the war and criticism fell silent for some years.

Pastoral Scene, 1859 – 1862. Ink, pencil and bistre. (2³/8 x 3⁹/16″) Present whereabouts unknown.

Around a Table in the Garden, c. 1868. Pastel, white gouache and pencil. (8¹/₄ x 11″) Present whereabouts unknown.

*Photograph of Cézanne talking
with Gaston Bernheim de Villers,
taken at Aix-en-Provence about 1904.*

Cézanne Criticism
After 1920

THE MOOD of the 1920s was very different from that of pre-1914 days: it brought a reaction against creative boldness and a return to academic positions. This change of taste had two consequences for Cézanne: his influence underwent an eclipse, as the painter Simon Lévy noted in a letter of 1920 to André Salmon[1]; and interpretations of his art emphasized its classical character.

This way of looking at Cézanne was shared even by the subtlest, most thoughtful writers. A typical example is that of C.F. Ramuz.[2] Writing in 1914, he saw that Cézanne had gone beyond Impressionism but believed that his participation in Impressionism had been a mistake rather than an advantage. He is right in his observations on Cé-zanne's character, on his humility, his "gaucherie" as an earnest of his sincerity, his inability as a painter to profit by what he had learned, his utter dedication to his art. But in his conviction that Cézanne was a classicist and traditionalist Ramuz reflects the taste of his time.

In 1921 appeared the monograph by Joachim Gasquet,[3] who as a boy had seen him painting in the Aix countryside, who knew him personally and was on something like familiar terms with him. One might have expected a definitive portrait of the artist, but Gasquet's imagination as a literary man and his defective historical sense led him to write the romance rather than the history of Cézanne. Half the book consists of alleged quotations from the master's talk, from his "lesson": "I am more traditional than people think... I am a classicist; I tell myself, I should like to be a classic... Imagine Poussin done over again entirely from nature, that is the classicism I mean."

No doubt Gasquet is sincere in his desire to be objective, and the book does ring true at times, as when Cézanne extols Veronese and Tintoretto or declares that the primitives do not interest him. Nevertheless, there is a difference between the personality emanating from Cézanne's letters and the personality reconstructed by Gasquet. As for the character of the man himself, Gasquet makes it out much more odd and dramatic than it can have been in reality.

The first to attempt a reconstitution of Cézanne's personality by studying the background, the works and the development of his style, with an art historian's sense of responsibility and the insight of a psychologist, was Roger Fry.[4] For him, Cézanne is closer to Poussin than to the Salon d'Automne, he is not decorative and not forcible, without emphasis or vivacity or perfection, but discreet, uncertain for fear of arrogance, and humble, rejecting all accepted knowledge so that conviction may arise gradually from the brushwork and contemplation. Cézanne's synthesis was a tendency, a reality never fully realized.

All this applies to Cézanne's maturity, not to his youth. The young Cézanne, Fry continues, was a violent revolutionary, a visionary more beholden to Delacroix than to Manet. His figure compositions were painted from imagination, without models; even though the colour is always the direct expression of form, they are unsuccessful because he lacked a sense of illustration and a sense of proportions. No primitive, Cézanne in his youth was a baroque artist who followed his inward passion, without the control that a grasp of external reality can give. His complex gifts were thus starkly revealed, out of the painter's heroic sincerity towards his own art. The pride, the will to conquer, of those early days gave way after 1870 to a great humility towards nature, under the effect of Pissarro's teaching and Impressionism. But he remained intent on the expression of volume, on chromatic harmony, on logical, architectonic design: in this he distinguished himself from the Impressionists. His still lifes soon achieved perfection, not only in their pictorial organization but in their power of expressing the artist's dramatic, noble, lyrical emotion. They are dramas without dramatic incidents. Cézanne's distortions are not wilful, but required by the overall harmony. He succeeds in imparting vitality even to abstract forms, and to the general design rhythmic phrasing gives momentum and direction. Witness the repose and the life, the Homeric solemnity, of *The Card Players*. Even the colour is geometric. Cézanne is a classicist, in the sense that every classicist has overcome the romantic within him.

The essential value of Roger Fry's study lies in the psychological analysis of Cézanne's form, in his understanding of the relation between intellectual structure and keenness of sensation. Perhaps its limitation lies in the emphasis on the traditional character of Cézanne's art, placing him on a level with the great masters of the past and so understating his kinship with the taste of his time. Fry, moreover, is apt to read failings into what are only peculiarities.

Henri Focillon in 1928[5] and Giorgio Castelfranco in 1934[6] made some apt observations which helped towards an understanding of Cézanne's art. Eugenio d'Ors,[7] however, projects into Cézanne his own classicist theory of the latter's art, so making a travesty of it.

In 1936 I published the first catalogue of Cézanne's work.[8] Illustrating 1,619 paintings, watercolours and drawings, several hundred of which had

Portrait of Joachim Gasquet, 1896–1897. Oil. (25³/4 x 21¹/2″) National Gallery, Prague.

never been reproduced, it provided a comprehensive view of his art that had not been available before. The chronological order adopted for this catalogue aroused some criticism, but it was the first attempt to trace the historical development of Cézanne's style and laid a basis for subsequent studies. The critical essay preceding the catalogue was an attempt to study Cézanne's evolution on its own terms, disregarding the developments that followed after his death and disregarding the polemics that still persisted in 1936.

My purpose was to combat several misconceptions: the still too common view of Cézanne as a precursor and therefore an incomplete artist; the overemphasis on his form to the detriment of colour, on his fidelity to tradition rather than his achievement as a renovator.

It was easy enough to draw a contrast between Cézanne's volumes and architecture and the impressionist disintegration of form. But this is to overlook certain facts. It was Pissarro, in initiating him into Impressionism, who helped him to arrive at the structural solidity that Cézanne lacked before 1870. For this reason I insisted on the importance of his impressionist experience, in opposition to the views of Roger Fry. I insisted on some further points: the necessity in his eyes of distorting form in order to achieve unity of style; his keen interest in art theory; the independence of his creative fantasy from his inventive imagination; his elimination of the subject in favour of the motif; his use of colour modulation instead of modelling.

Meanwhile our knowledge of Cézanne's life was being notably extended, first by Gerstle Mack's biography in 1935,[9] then by John Rewald's edition of the letters in 1937,[10] followed by several essays by Rewald and then by his Cézanne monograph of 1939,[11] rich in new material and throwing light in particular on Cézanne's relations with Zola.

An important contribution to Cézanne criticism was made in 1937 by Fritz Novotny.[12] He laid stress on the artist's rejection of psychological expression, his use of a perspective devoid of any emotional content, and the soundness of his figural and spatial structure despite the seeming immateriality of the objects represented. Colour creates the object, and so the contour of a figure is not so much the limit of an object as a relation of chromatic elements with the picture as a whole. This rules out the modelling of form in favour of colour modulation. Cézanne's art is in effect pure painting, a creation radically distinct from nature.

During the war, in 1943, the University of California Press published Erle Loran's essay on *Cézanne's Composition*. Himself a painter, Loran had made a long study of Cézanne's painting, deducing from it some general principles of art theory. This is not in my view the best approach to art criticism, but Loran's diagrams of Cézanne paintings do bring out some of his essential qualities: the importance of the picture plane, the dynamism of his forms, the transformation of natural perspective by the regrouping of volumes, thus creating a new relation between the picture plane and three-dimensional vision. Loran's main point is his demonstration that the objects in a Cézanne painting are sometimes defined from different points of view, so as to contrast the real planes with imaginary planes and convey the impression of a greater complexity of volume and space than exists in reality. The distortions are thus deliberately made in order to heighten the dramatic character of the representation.

After the Second World War Cézanne studies continued and grew. Bernard Dorival[13] in 1948 published an extensive monograph in which he reconsidered the complex problems raised by Cézanne's art, focusing attention on the contradictions which the artist strove to overcome. The unity of his work was seen as a fusion of opposites achieved in the successive phases of his style: concrete and imaginative, intellectual and sensory, baroque and classical, atmospheric vibration and architectonic construction.

Liliane Guerry[14] made a careful and searching analysis of the development of spatial representation in Cézanne: the first artificial attempts before 1870; the persistent efforts to erect a spatial container in his impressionist years; the synthetic reconstruction of space in the years 1879–1895; and finally the achievement of a supreme harmony in the last works where container and contained are fused in a created space of his own.

Pierre Francastel[15] singled out Cézanne's power of transforming objects into things of wider scope and meaning. His *Château Noir* is not just a house but something that one loves, desires and can acquire; it stands in a space at once concrete and imaginary. *The Card Players* are no longer men of the people, testifying to more or less acrimonious or romantic demands; they are considered for their own sake as self-evident material for art. And so the "subject" disappeared.

Meyer Schapiro in 1952[16] made an acute study of the abstract side of Cézanne's art, his artistic reconstruction of reality. Rather than colour, it was his brushwork that opened the way to abstraction. Instead of reaching any definite conclusion, his art was a continuous experiment and development. His order was never calculated but varied according as his mood tended towards the serene or the dramatic. Instead of being diffused over the objects represented, light was the very basis of the visual sensations by which he was able to reconstruct a stable world rich in colour. By choosing a landscape in which man has no place, he attained that contemplative calm which is a suspension of all desire.

Even the still lifes are imbued with this detachment, which makes them objects of contemplation. Even in some of the portraits, and always in the figure groups of bathers, this contemplative detachment is evident; hence the lack of psychological expression. The pictures of card players exemplify this timeless moment of pure contemplation, of thought without action. This weight of thought and this detachment from desire are the essential characteristics of Cézanne's art. His distortions arise from the influence of emotion on his perceptions and from the effort to achieve a full equilibrium and harmony of forms. "The way in which these objects take on life thanks to Cézanne's perceptions and his constructive operations is more fascinating than their meaning or their relation to our desires." The importance of Meyer Schapiro's essay lies in the emphasis he puts on Cézanne's creative process rather than on the result achieved; and not only is this very helpful for an understanding of Cézanne, but it represents a new general principle of art criticism.

Lawrence Gowing[17] spoke of Cézanne in passionate accents, because for him the fine purity of the artist's form and architecture imparted a new depth of human meaning to the subject. His art is an insight into the unity of the real world, gradually revealed through a system of analogies and correspondences. The style of the last years he likened to an embrace of nature, a recreation of a beloved object.

A systematic review of the many problems and themes of Cézanne criticism was made by Kurt Badt,[18] and supplemented shortly afterwards by Gertrude Berthold.[19] Badt traced the relations between Cézanne and the masters who had preceded him, using the historical method which had been adopted for modern painting by Meier-Graefe many years before. For Badt, Cézanne represented a synthesis of Poussin and Delacroix, and he owed more to the influence of Courbet's "realism" than to Manet's "naturalism." In the style of Cézanne's last years he saw an identity between the detail and the whole, which he explained as the outcome of the freedom of the picture elements within the freedom of the picture as a whole. Besides the connection with earlier masters, Badt finely brought out the symbolism, humanity and modernity of Cézanne in relation to the social conditions of the nineteenth century. This is certainly the widest-ranging study of Cézanne from the historical (as against the critical and aesthetic) point of view.

As to the future, new insights are always possible, and it may be expected that some new conclusions will be drawn from such works as are yet unpublished. What is clear is that, thanks to the efforts of many students of Cézanne, his personality has been clarified and his historical position defined. Above all, the image of Cézanne has for decades now stood free of the controversies that raged around him, and he has taken the eminent place that is his due in the history of art in the nineteenth century.

A Card Player, 1892–1896. Pencil. (19¹/₄ x 15³/₄")
Present whereabouts unknown.

The Card Players, 1890–1892. Oil. (25½ x 32″) The Metropolitan Museum of Art, New York. Gift of Stephen C. Clark.

Photograph of Aix-en-Provence.

3

Cézanne as a Romantic

ÉZANNE'S early style shows some Provençal characteristics which must be taken into account. The first painter to exert an influence on him appears to have been Emile Loubon. Born in Aix in 1809, Loubon was in Paris for a time, in contact with Decamps and Troyon; he then settled in Marseilles where as director of the school of fine arts he diffused his romantic tastes. Of the pictures he painted in Marseilles, two entered the Aix museum: *The Raising of the "Camp du Midi"* (1855) and *Rams at the Head of a Herd in Camargue* (1853). His thick impasto and his dark, turbulent, violently contrasting colours are reminiscent of those of the early Cézanne. There is a connection too in their subjects, Loubon having painted some views of the bay of Marseilles which, as far as the motif goes, are similar to Cézanne's views of L'Estaque—the latter of course being painted with a far greater intensity and mastery. Loubon furthermore had been looked up to as a leader by that group of Provençal painters which included Monticelli, who was a friend of Cézanne's.

One of the most significant Provençal artists who showed some kinship with Cézanne was Paul Guigou, who died in 1871 at the age of only thirty-seven; he was a friend of Monticelli's and a protégé of Loubon's. It is not known for certain whether Cézanne and Guigou ever met, nor is it possible to say whether either influenced the other. What we do know is that Guigou went to Paris to study Courbet and that Cézanne never made any secret of his admiration for Courbet. Cézanne and Guigou were actuated by the same desire for realism, both approaching it with romantic prepossessions. They aimed at contrasts of light, and Guigou's colour early reached a high pitch of brightness; both were intent on bringing out in the Provençal landscape that harmony and architectonic power which is characteristic of both their styles. Cézanne, however, proceeded more slowly than Guigou, and went more deeply into things, with a romantic ardour typical of his character—that ardour for which he did not succeed in achieving a corresponding form until later, after 1865.

Another painter from Provence must have exerted some influence on Cézanne, in this case a great artist: Daumier.

Though schooled as an artist in Paris, Daumier was born in Marseilles and grew up there. From him Cézanne took over several subjects, like *The Donkey and the Thieves* and *The Murder*, both painted before 1870. But it is above all in their outlook on life and the world that one sees a kinship between the two artists. If one takes Delacroix as the foremost painter of the romantic school and Courbet as the foremost realist, Daumier is seen to represent a synthesis of

François-Marius Granet (1775–1849). Terrace of the Artist's Country House at Le Malvalat near Aix, c. 1830. Oil. (12¹/2 x 9⁵/8″) Musée Granet, Aix-en-Provence.

Paul Guigou (1834–1871).
Landscape in Provence: View of St-Saturnin-lès-Apt, 1867. Oil. (10⁷/8 x 18″)
Musée du Petit Palais, Paris.

The Donkey and the Thieves, 1869–1870. Oil.
(16¹/₈ x 21⁵/₈″) Civica Galleria d'Arte Moderna, Milan.

romanticism and realism; for Daumier was also a Provençal realist, full of ardour and passion. Thus Cézanne was too much of a poet to remain prosaically attached to the realism of Courbet, and at the same time too headstrong to be content with assimilating Manet's way of seeing.

Already in his early works, then, Cézanne was laying the foundations of his artistic and poetic vision: a concrete world of his own, deeply rooted in his native Provence but invested with a passionate romanticism, magnified and transposed beyond reality by the power of his imagination. But in order to strike a balance between this inner passion and his outward expression of it, Cézanne had to work out a much more complex style than that of his youth, a style compounded of something more than elementary contrasts of light and pre-expressionist distortions of reality. He had in the first place to enrich his palette; his colour had to take on those gleaming vibrations which only the discoveries of the Impressionists enabled him to achieve. Only after he had assimilated the lesson of Impressionism was he able to create a monumental painting of his own, solidly based on the landscape architecture of his native Provence.

The Murder, 1867–1870. Oil. (25¹/₄ x 31⁷/₈″) Walker Art Gallery, Liverpool.

Portrait of Eugène Delacroix, 1864–1866. Pencil and soft crayon. (5¹/₂ x 5¹/₈″) Musée Calvet, Avignon.

Copy of Delacroix's "Medea Slaying her Children," 1879–1882. Watercolour. (15 x 9⁷/₈″) Kunsthaus, Zürich.

The two painters who cast the most potent spell over Cézanne were Delacroix and Courbet. So great was his veneration for the former that in his last years Cézanne planned an *Apotheosis of Delacroix;* and his reinterpretations of Delacroix's *Barque of Dante, Medea* and *Hagar in the Desert* prove how often he referred to him. But his *Hamlet and Horatio* after Delacroix also shows how original was his rehandling of him: its expressive power derives not from the action of the figures but from the violent movement of the images, as if shaken by a winter wind, and from the forceful contrast of blue and orange tones. This little picture was painted as late as the 1870s; it represents the stage he had then arrived at in the break-up of form, before reconstructing it under the impact of Impressionism.

Joachim Gasquet[1] records a conversation with Cézanne in which the latter had this to say of Delacroix: "One may speak of him, even after Tintoretto and Rubens, without having to blush... He remains the finest palette in France, and no one more than he, under our skies... has had the calmness and emotion at once, the vibration of colour. We all of us paint like him, as all of you write like Hugo."

The influence of Courbet was probably stronger, even though it served rather to moderate an excess of romanticism. Pictures like *The Outing* and *Conversation* were obviously inspired by Courbet. Often in Cézanne's way of shading colours, without weakening their intensity, there lingers a memory of Courbet. Despite these points of contact, Cézanne's grasp and practice of painting was profoundly different; so much so that even that strenuous handling of the pigments, most evident around 1865, which made for a certain kinship with Courbet at that time, was soon transformed into an intensely personal power and mastery over colour and its vibrations. Manet too, who in 1863 had painted the *Déjeuner sur l'Herbe* and *Olympia*, contributed to Cézanne's early development, despite the great difference of temperament and vision between them.

About 1865, rebelling against all that he had learned in the schools and museums, Cézanne gained a confused awareness of what he was after. He was not yet painting in the open air, not yet looking to nature: it was the inner revolution of an artist who expressed the fury of his revolt, not so much in his subjects, as in his form and in his way of painting with the palette knife. For the brush and its

Adolphe Monticelli (1824–1886).
Two Women in a Garden, c. 1873–1875.
Oil. (18½ x 14½")
Musée Granet, Aix-en-Provence.

Conversation, 1870–1871.
Oil. (36¼ x 28¾")
Private Collection, Paris.

Déjeuner sur l'Herbe (Luncheon on the Grass), 1869–1870. Oil. (23⁵/₈ x 31⁷/₈") Private Collection, Paris.

A Modern Olympia, 1870. Oil. (22 x 21⅝")
Private Collection, Paris.

refinements he substituted the bricklayer's trowel. It was precisely by spreading on the colour, not through chiaroscuro, that he created his plastic form, building it up in masses, powerfully and rudely shaped, conceived as if meant to be seen from a distance, and executed as if meant to be seen at close range, indeed calling for the touch of the hand. The discrepancy between conception and execution may detract from the artistic result but opens the way, forty years in advance, to that creative tension peculiar to the art of our century.

So radical is the fragmentation of the brushwork and the synthesis of forms that the *Girl at the Piano (Overture of Tannhäuser)* foreshadows the Matisse of 1905. But this boldness was still exceptional. More typical of his output of 1865–1868 is the series of

portraits of "Uncle Dominique," the best of which is probably the one in the Metropolitan Museum, New York. This painting is justified by the energy with which he invests the subject, by the thickness he gives to form not merely with the brush but with the palette knife which imparts an added intensity to the colour and suggests volume even though he resorts to no contrasts of light and no chiaroscuro effects. And though the expression of space is not yet attempted (he did not come to grips with the space-colour problem until he had absorbed the lesson of Impressionism), the image is substantial, forceful and successfully synthesized.

At this time, in the 1860s, Cézanne believed that he could achieve volume through the thickness of his pigments, taking his cue in this from Courbet; and he believed he could replace light effects by the gleaming preciosity of his pigments, in this parting company with Courbet. The same concern appears in other pictures of this period, which are more turbulent in their unrestrained sensuality and the expansive urge he felt towards the spectacular: *The Orgy, The Temptation of St Anthony* and *The Pastoral*. In *The Orgy* the pigments are rich and glowing, but without any effect of light or atmosphere. In *The Temptation* the strain of sensuality runs less deep, so completely is passion concentrated in the contrasts of light and shadow. *The Pastoral* draws its poetry from the participation of things, on earth and in the heavens, from a drama without action, an agitation that is purely pictorial. Cézanne shares too impetuously in the life of his images; for him there was no thought of detachment or contemplation. This attitude stemmed from his approach to reality. He believed himself to be a realist; his preferences among the painters of the past (Zurbaran) and those of the present (Courbet) are indicative of that assumption. But what did reality mean to Cézanne at this time? Certainly it did not mean what it

Man with a Nightcap (Uncle Dominique), 1865. Oil. ($31^{3}/_{8}$ x $25^{1}/_{4}$") The Metropolitan Museum of Art, New York.

Melting Snow at L'Estaque, c. 1870. Oil. (28³/₄ x 36¹/₄")
Private Collection, Paris.

The Orgy, 1864–1868. Oil. (51¹/₈ x 31⁷/₈")
Private Collection, Paris.

meant to Courbet, whose realism consisted in taking over from nature such features as could best be turned into painting. The realism of Cézanne was at bottom formless; it was the mental superstructure of a passionate, strongly introverted temperament; it was a romantic transformation of reality. But to achieve complete possession of that reality, Cézanne soon found that he would have to attenuate his romanticism and take a broader approach to nature, opening his whole mind and eyes to the life of nature—in other words, surrendering himself to it as the Impressionists had done.

The positive side of his activity between 1865 and 1870 lay in breaking decisively with his academic schooling and the misguided enthusiasms of his first sojourn in Paris. Cabanel and Meissonier were forgotten, and he henceforth constructed his pictures by breaking up plastic form and thus opening it to light; this enabled him to substitute colour modulation for modelling. Witness his *Melting Snow at*

L'Estaque of about 1870. Though it is still romantic in spirit, the composition does not rest on a pattern of design; instead, it is built up in terms of chromatic masses. Cézanne now was ready to endorse the lesson of the Impressionists and to use colour as a constructive element, resorted to not only for its contrasts of tones but for its blendings and vibrations, for the broken touch and transparencies which transform the suggestion of volume into a real sense of volume. Thus, to give life to the image, he no longer needed to increase the thickness of his pigments, which for all their refinements had remained subdued. He depended now on chromatic construction; or, as he later called it when distinguishing his picture structure from that of the schools, on construction by tones.

Pencil study for "Pastoral," c. 1870. (4 x 5¹/₄")
Henry Pearlman Estate, New York.

Pastoral (Don Quixote on the Barbary Coast), 1870.
Oil. (25¹/₂ x 31⁷/₈") Private Collection, Paris.

Camille Pissarro (1830–1903).
The Diligence at Louveciennes, 1870.
Oil. (10 x 14″) Louvre, Paris.

An initial result of this approach is *The Black Clock* (1869–1871). For all its impasto, as thick as in the previous works, it was painted with the brush, not the palette knife, so that the tones are more transparent and the chromatic unity is achieved by a finer vibration of the colour and atmosphere. Space too, being more accurately defined, has become more palpable; no longer a backdrop setting off a still life, it is an organic part of the composition having the same pictorial intensity, that is the same emotional intensity, as the other elements. The scale of colours, however, is still restricted, darker tones still predominating in contrast with the white tablecloth in the foreground; but the light in which these tones are steeped makes them finer and richer.

The Black Clock is important not only for its technique and the way of applying the colours, but also because it testifies to a new conception of reality, no longer expressed as intense romantic emotion, but steadied and deepened into an emotion inherent in the form itself, in the volumes that stand firm and distinct before us.

The years between 1863 and 1870 saw the first impressionist works of the painters whom Cézanne had met in Paris and at the Académie Suisse. Indeed this fruitful period of ferment and preparation had already produced some masterpieces: Manet's *Olympia* and *Le Déjeuner sur l'Herbe*, Pissarro's pictures of Bougival, and Renoir's and Monet's pictures of *La Grenouillère* in which the impressionist way of seeing advances beyond the experimental phase and becomes style. Cézanne's *Black Clock* cannot be called an impressionist painting, but it represents an advance parallel to that of Impressionism.

Claude Monet (1840–1926).
La Grenouillère, 1869. Oil. (29³/₈ x 39³/₈″)
The Metropolitan Museum of Art, New York.
The H.O. Havemeyer Collection, 1929.

Auguste Renoir (1841–1919).
La Grenouillère, 1869. Oil. (26 x 31⁷/₈″)
National Museum, Stockholm.

The Black Clock, 1869–1871. Oil. (21⁵/8 x 29¹/2″) Collection Stavros S. Niarchos, Paris.

The House of Dr. Gachet at Auvers-sur-Oise, c. 1873. Oil. (18¹/₈ x 15″) Galerie du Jeu de Paume, Louvre, Paris.

4

Impressionism

Self-Portrait, 1873–1874. Oil. (25¹/4 x 20⁷/8″)
Louvre, Paris.

THE FRANCO-PRUSSIAN War of 1870 scattered the artists, but they soon came together again in 1871 after the Commune. In 1872–1873 Cézanne was at Pontoise and Auvers-sur-Oise, to the northwest of Paris, where he painted in the open air with Pissarro, in the Vexin countryside near the river Oise where the atmosphere was vibrant with light and the landscape rich in fine shades of colour. From this time on, he set himself to paint what he saw before him, and the concentrated effort to do so cured him of literary leanings, storytelling, subject painting and dramatic emotivity at any price. External nature assumed in his work a prominent enough place to balance the ferment of his inner passion.

Cézanne had worked before in the open air; in a letter of 1868 he speaks of a landscape he was painting on the banks of the river Arc, near Aix, which he intended to submit to the 1869 Salon. But he had never yet gone beyond the stage represented by *Melting Snow at L'Estaque*. Looking at the landscapes painted after 1871, like *The House and the Tree*, which shows Dr. Gachet's house at Auvers, or *The Hanged Man's House at Auvers*, which is one of Cézanne's masterpieces, it is clear at once that the landscape is no longer seen as a contrast of forms and muted colours. The tones are handled with complete freedom and he builds up the picture in terms of colour. In other words, he had been won over to the impressionist way of seeing.

A Modern Olympia, 1872–1873. Oil. (18¹/₈ x 21⁵/₈")
Galerie du Jeu de Paume, Louvre, Paris.

Cézanne owed this new maturity to Pissarro, who taught him to look at reality with a certain detachment and made him understand that it could be rendered through his own temperament and in the mood of a particular moment, without investing it with all the loves and hates of his own character. If there must be dramatic overtones, they should be those of the light and shadow; they should lie in the pictorial means, not in a literary adjunct. Pissarro encouraged him to follow up the path which he had taken with *The Black Clock*, but which could not yield results until he had gained a greater freedom and above all a greater complexity in the colour effect. Of all the Impressionists, Pissarro was the one most intent on pictorial construction, on a structural synthesis of light itself. This is probably the main reason why the two men got on so well together, their association stimulating Cézanne in his search for monumentality. While admiring Monet and appreciating his work very much (whatever legend would subsequently say to the contrary),

Cézanne had nothing in common with him: he and Monet represented two completely different conceptions of painting—one, Cézanne's, developing into Cubism; the other, Monet's, developing into Fauvism.

For Cézanne, impressionist light meant above all construction, space-colour, a synthesis of volumes. And this preoccupation appears now not only in the landscapes but also the interiors; for example, in *A Modern Olympia* (1872–1873), which is handled much more freely than the earlier version (1870). The darker tones of old linger in only a few details: the figure of the artist, his hat, his dog. The rest is vibrant and glowing, a rhythm of bright colours extending from the red table on the left to the greens interwoven with yellow, blue and red of the large bouquet on the upper right.

The Hanged Man's House at Auvers is an accomplished example of the new direction taken by Cézanne and even anticipates his later experiments, when he had moved beyond Impressionism. While space is no longer amorphous, the vibration of light, obtained despite the usual impasto, makes it almost compact, like a mass which has body but not excessive weight, thanks to the delicacy of the landscape elements. It is light that creates this synthesis of volume and space, a synthesis which gives to things the sense of eternity; or better perhaps (to use a concept which will be necessary to judge the late works), the sense of their *actual duration* as it impinges on the mind. Here Cézanne wedded his own vision of monumentality and grandeur to the structural soundness he had learned from Pissarro; and naturally he goes beyond that structure because he is not satisfied with a purely optical dimension of his images—already he is in search of an emotional dimension of form. So one can understand, even if one cannot justify, the error made by those, beginning with Emile Bernard, who saw in Cézanne the

The Hanged Man's House at Auvers-sur-Oise, 1872–1873. Oil. (21⁵/₈ x 26″) Galerie du Jeu de Paume, Louvre, Paris.

Head of a Girl, 1873.
Etching. (5¹/4 x 4¹/4")

Self-Portrait of the Artist Etching beside
Dr. Gachet, 1873. Pencil. (8¹/16 x 5³/16")
Louvre, Paris.

Portrait of Dr. Gachet,
c. 1873. Charcoal. (12¹¹/16 x 8¹/2")
Cabinet des Dessins, Louvre, Paris.

restorer of a classical order (for Bernard, a neo-classical order), and by those who denied that Cézanne had ever been an Impressionist. It is an error that cannot be justified because, if Cézanne attained to structure, volume and colour mass, it was thanks to a knowledge of colour which he had not possessed before, and thanks to that detachment from reality, turned now into a motif instead of a subject, which was one of the main conquests of Impressionism.

That he himself was satisfied with the new direction he had given his work by 1874 is proved by the letter to his mother of 26 September 1874 (see page 33), and by the fact that he took part in the first group exhibition of the painters who were to be dubbed Impressionists. Pissarro, Renoir and Monet, to mention only the greatest among them, held Cézanne in the highest esteem. Comparing his works of this period with those of the other Impressionists, and of Pissarro himself, one realizes that

Cézanne had fully assimilated the lesson of Impressionism, had taken over its way of seeing and technique; yet his conception of it was so different that he arrived at wholly personal results, at a commanding force and grandeur of vision that carried well beyond merely physical appearances.

One need only look at a still life (V. 185 for example) contemporary with the Auvers landscapes or the *Bouquet in a Delft Vase* (Louvre, Paris) to feel that, in Cézanne's hands, the vibration of colour and light does not serve to sensitize form but to make it more compact and evident, to define the planes in order to bring out volumes more forcibly. Yet in the *Bouquet in a Delft Vase* the colour is no longer treated according to elementary accords and contrasts, but is set forth with all the wealth of the impressionist palette; and in the still life just cited, objects and background are fused in a single unifying atmosphere.

Bouquet in a Delft Vase, c. 1873–1875. Oil. (16¹/8 x 10⁵/8″)
Galerie du Jeu de Paume, Louvre, Paris.

The Surrounding Wall, 1875–1876. Oil. (19³/4 x 25⁵/8″) Present whereabouts unknown.

After 1877, when he ceased to take part in the group exhibitions, he justified his abstention on theoretical grounds: he felt the need, he said, to stand aloof in order to see his way forward more clearly. But even when he developed his style towards the construction of form, while the Impressionists themselves pressed on in directions of their own, Cézanne never forgot the lesson he had learned from Impressionism. Even his famous statement of his aim, to "vivify Poussin from nature,"[1] probably originated in his experience of Impressionism.

It is interesting to find Cézanne expressing the desire to "defend theoretically"[2] his way of painting, for this points to an aspect of his temperament which sets him apart from most of his painter friends. He was a man who thought, and thought profoundly, about his art; he was not one who surrendered to the joy of painting. If he worked out and amplified a vision of his own, it was thanks to hard work and perseverance; if the mastery he acquired cost him so many pains, it was not from lack of ability but from an unremitting desire to do still better. But like the Impressionists he experienced the rapture of colour; in an undated letter to his old Aixois friend Marius Roux, of about 1877 or shortly before, he refers to his "little personality as an impressionist painter."[3]

To 1872 or 1873 can be traced back Cézanne's desire to develop a brushstroke that should be, not merely responsive to the nuances of nature, but form-creating. *The Surrounding Wall*, painted about 1875–1876, shows that the impressionist way of seeing had been completely assimilated, together with the impressionist way of painting. The colours are

Photograph of Camille Pissarro (left) and Paul Cézanne (right) at Auvers-sur-Oise, between 1872 and 1876.

Pissarro Going out to Paint in the Open Air, 1872–1876. Pencil. (7¹¹/₁₆ x 4⁷/₁₆") Cabinet des Dessins, Louvre, Paris.

applied in short separate touches, running in different directions so as to enable the reflections to fuse lights and colours in each touch. The wall is purplish-blue, with blue reflections cast by the trees; the meadow is green, the ground greenish-yellow, the tree-trunks grey or brownish-grey, the foliage green with one yellow branch, the roofs red and the sky grey. Spatial recession is obtained almost wholly by means of colours more or less steeped in atmosphere. In short, everything in this picture is consonant with Impressionism, nor does even the sense of grandeur peculiar to Cézanne run counter to it.

It was only to be expected that during his impressionist period Cézanne would paint chiefly landscapes. But he also produced some still lifes, which helped him to define and perfect his way of seeing. And he painted some portraits too, one of the finest being that of Victor Chocquet of 1876–1877, which reveals the deeper human insight that Cézanne had gained from Impressionism. Hair, beard, blue-grey jacket, bluish-white shirt and reddish flesh-tints stand out against a light green ground; an effect, then, of dark on light. The brushstrokes, though thick with pigment, are so varied as to set the light vibrating, as if indeed light itself went to form the image. From this flawless unity of form and colour arises the likeness of the man and patron dear to both Cézanne and Renoir—a man sensitive, serious, strong-willed, acquainted with suffering, and living a deep inner life of his own. The work of art and the representation of a human life are fused, thanks to the flow of sympathy and interest between artist and sitter, and to Cézanne's response to spiritual values as well as to natural objects.

Of course, if Cézanne was able to convey all this, it is because he now had a definite vision of his own and the technique to embody it. The picture construction is highly skilled and summons up a commanding presence. It is no longer a surface pattern,

Auguste Renoir (1841–1919). Portrait of Victor Chocquet, 1876. Oil. (18 1/8 x 14 1/8″) Collection Oskar Reinhart am Römerholz, Winterthur, Switzerland.

as in the series of portraits of *Uncle Dominique*, but a construction in depth set up by the rhythm of light and shadow; after breaking down the apparent structure of the colour, Cézanne recreates the image by working out a new structure that is not only material but spiritual, its internal tension deriving from the mind.

Cézanne by now had got the full benefit of Impressionism, and before him opened a prospect of boundless possibilities. The work accomplished in the space of ten years had been great and fruitful, and it included some of his masterpieces.

Portrait of Victor Chocquet, 1876–1877. Oil. (18¹/₈ x 14¹/₈″) Private Collection.

1. *Head of Madame Cézanne and Milk Can,*
   1877–1880. Pencil. (9¹/16 x 5⁷/8″)
   Collection Lord Clark, London.

2. *Sheet of Studies with a Clock, 1876–1879. Pencil.*
   (9⁵/8 x 12″) Collection E. Katzenellenbogen,
   Santa Monica, California.

3. *Head of the Artist's Son Paul Asleep,*
   c. 1877. Pencil. (6⁵/16 x 9¹/4″)
   Collection Lord Clark, London.

4. *Sheet of Studies with Madame Cézanne Sewing*
   and Victor Chocquet, 1877–1880. Pencil.
   (7³/4 x 9¹/8″) Collection of Mr. and Mrs.
   Benjamin Sonnenberg, New York.

5. *Two Female Heads, 1883–1886. Pencil.*
   (7⁵/8 x 4⁵/8″) Private Collection, Paris.

6. *Three Heads of the Artist's Son Paul Asleep,*
   1878–1880. Pencil. (14 x 19³/8″)
   Collection Lord Clark, London.

7. *Three Heads of Paul and Studies after Pedro*
   de Moya and Tintoretto, 1879–1880. Pencil.
   (9⁷/16 x 12³/16″) The Lazarus and Rosalie
   Phillips Family Collection, Montreal.

8. *Sheet of Studies with Spirit Lamp,*
   1880–1883. Pencil. (9⁷/16 x 12³/16″)
   Collection Oswald T. Falk, Oxford.

9. *Head of Madame Cézanne, 1888–1891.*
   Pencil. (5⁷/8 x 4³/4″)
   Collection W.S. Schiess, Basel.

10. *Head of Madame Cézanne, c. 1880.*
    Pencil. (6³/4 x 4³/4″) Private Collection, Paris.

11. *Madame Cézanne Sewing, c. 1880.*
    Pencil. (18⁷/8 x 12³/8″)
    Collection Paul Cassirer, Amsterdam.

12. *Portrait of Madame Cézanne, 1887–1890.*
    Pencil. (19¹/16 x 12¹¹/16″)
    Boymans-van Beuningen Museum, Rotterdam.

13. *Self-Portrait, c. 1880. Pencil.*
    (13 x 10³/4″) The Metropolitan Museum of Art,
    New York. Bequest of Walter C. Baker.

1

2

11

10

81

Still Life with Apples, Bottle and Soup Tureen, 1883–1885. Oil. (25⁵/₈ x 32¹/₈″) Galerie du Jeu de Paume, Louvre, Paris.

Self-Portrait, 1879–1882. Oil. (24 x 20")
Kunstmuseum, Berne.

5

Plastic Construction

IN THE DECADE after 1877 Cézanne worked his way towards a new plastic organization of forms in which the structure of the images, whether figures, landscapes or still lifes, became ever more volumetric and more abstract. Pissarro, likewise concerned with solidity of form, arrived at a sound, organic construction of the picture. Impressionism itself entered a time of crisis in the late 1870s and all the artists who had contributed to its creation turned towards other lines of research.

Light, in its play and effects, was no longer considered to be all-sufficing; and even when it remained the principal picture element, as in Monet after 1884, it assumed a different function. It went to define a form which was no longer impressionist, no longer determined by the atmospheric vibra-

tion or by the fusion or division of the brushstrokes. Instead of dissolving in depth, the image tended to stand out on the picture surface, with an effect of abstraction which anticipated, on the one hand, Monet's own abandonment of figurative painting and, on the other, that "shock of colour on our senses" which came with the Fauves twenty years later. Renoir, after a trip to Rome, turned his attention to a form deriving from Ingres or Raphael which had a mortifying effect on his colour for nearly ten years—after which he reverted to it with fresh ardour. Pissarro himself, in his desire to seat Impressionism on new and firmer foundations, fell in with the scientific ideas of Seurat, whose "pointillism" also represented a structural method. The fact is that the art of these last fifteen years of the

Auguste Renoir (1841–1919). The Large Bathers, 1884–1887. Oil. (45¹/₄ x 67″) Philadelphia Museum of Art.

Camille Pissarro (1830–1903).
L'Ile Lacroix, Rouen, Fog Effect, 1888.
Oil. (17¹/₄ x 21⁵/₈″)
Philadelphia Museum of Art.

nineteenth century laid the basis for the developments of the twentieth.

Cézanne, working in isolation from 1877 on, after the failure of the third impressionist exhibition, and ever more reluctant to exchange ideas with his friends, created in solitude what was to prove the major contribution to twentieth-century art. That he concentrated all his efforts on a better, sounder structure of the pictorial image is clear not only from his works but also, for example, from his judgments of Gauguin, in whom, obviously unable to understand him, he could see nothing but "Chinese images," and of Monet, whom he described as "only an eye"—this not being meant, however, in the disparaging sense that some have supposed, for he added: "but what an eye!" The mere sensation of things was not enough for Cézanne, nor did he aim at colour abstractions, nor by way of colour at a heightening of emotion. Abstraction for him could only be volumetric, and the image had to be intensified in its pictorial essence, not by an expressionistic distortion, but on the contrary by an ever more rigorous control of form.

Cézanne was the better prepared to exercise that control because he himself had practised, and then overcome, the habit of romantic-expressionist distortion of form in pictures like *The Pastoral*. Moreover, as late as 1873–1877 he had painted pictures of romantic inspiration like *The Temptation of St Anthony* in which there is a flagrant contradiction between the subject and the impressionist technique. It is true that in other paintings of that period, like the *Bathers at Rest* (Barnes Foundation, Merion, Pa.), the overwrought handling is tempered by the rigour of the composition.

Returning to L'Estaque in 1878, Cézanne worked hard, reacting resolutely against the discouragement that had come over him after the failure of the third group exhibition of the Impressionists in 1877. He continued to send in pictures to the official Salons, though well knowing that they would be refused. He did so, not from any thought of compromise, but to assert his own conviction that he was on the right path, whatever others might think.

At L'Estaque, on the Mediterranean, near Marseilles, he had before him the southern landscape that he loved, and Impressionism had now brought home to him the importance of working outdoors, directly from nature. That he should then proceed to transform the landscape before him, to adapt it to the requirements of his own art and sensibility, was his right and privilege as a great artist. And if he chose from the landscape the motifs best suited to his painting and did not aim at an overall vision of it, as a now effete realism would have required, this too was in the nature of things, in keeping with his conception of painting as, more and more, *presentation* and not *representation* (which, moreover, was also in keeping with the French landscape tradition from Valenciennes to Corot and beyond).

Not that he simply chose from nature the most beautiful elements, like an eclectic painter proceeding in the neo-classical manner. His purpose was to transmute the physical response to nature into a spiritual dimension of his own. Being deeply committed both morally and spiritually to his painting, he was far removed from anything in the way of neo-classical abstraction; his structural rhythms are dense and heaving, never a matter of static equilib-

rium and balanced masses. Cézanne's persistent search for a structural order in landscape shows that he did not mean to allow his effects of colour and light to be governed by any principle of abstract equilibrium. What he sought, on the contrary, was to build with colours and lights, to match order to visual sensation, and thus give its full significance to the chosen motif.

On his return to Provence in the late 1870s, his concern with structure appears clearly in several paintings of Provençal motifs which he finished about 1878. And above all in the watercolour *Landscape in Provence*: drawn in accordance with the traditional central perspective, the landscape is framed, is set off, by two clumps of trees forming two emphatically volumetric masses of colour; in the background rises the volume of a mountain, not a mere backdrop, but a compact mass which seems to concentrate and limit in a space vibrant with colour the entire landscape and the emotion it arouses.

Everything is built up with colour, for despite his concern with structural solidity he was not prepared to give up his chromatic vision. He did not draw,

Landscape with a Man Fishing, c. 1880. Pencil. (11 1/4 x 17 7/8")
Collection Lord Clark, London.

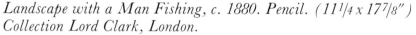

Landscape in Provence, 1875–1878. Watercolour. (14³/4 x 19¹/2″) Kunsthaus, Zürich.

he did not use a closed line or chiaroscuro effects. The design is chromatic; colour is not laid in over a form previously constructed, but what takes place is the immediate creation of a colour-form. This is further proof of the importance assumed by Impressionism in Cézanne's development, which can be seen to have proceeded steadily and gradually, without any violent break, as he pondered and enlarged on the experience gained.

When he was away from Provence, as he was for the most part between 1879 and 1882, he found in the landscapes of northern France similar motifs answering to the constructive order that he had in mind. The motif of a turning road, for example, is developed in several paintings of this period. The road assumes the character of a mounting path, but it is not the essential element of the composition, this being rather the sloping ground, trees and houses whose volumes surround and enclose it. Empty space is not represented but is suggested by contrast with the full-bodied forms. Cézanne thus discovered the plastic value of empty space.

Cézanne's constructive style gained force and conviction especially after his return to Aix, in the period between 1883 and 1887 when he seldom left Provence and remained in daily contact with the southern landscape, with its peculiar light and contrasts. In this period too he held aloof from his impressionist friends and took no part in their new experiments. And while he thought out his views on art and shaped them into a theory, he never envisaged them as a mental superstructure to his painting but always sought to apply his ideas to his art. Emile Bernard later recorded him as saying: "I confess that I am afraid of too much knowledge and that I prefer naïveté to knowledge."

Turning Road, 1879–1882. Oil. (23¹/2 x 28³/8″)
Courtesy of the Museum of Fine Arts, Boston.

Turning Road, 1879–1882. Oil. (18¹/2 x 21³/4″)
Collection of Mr. and Mrs. David Lloyd Kreeger, Washington. D.C.

Turning Road at La Roche-Guyon, c. 1885. Oil. (25¹/4 x 31¹/2″) Smith College Museum of Art, Northampton, Mass.

This hankering after primitivism found full expression in some of the paintings of 1882–1885, a period of ever greater structural emphasis in the pictorial image; for example, the well-known *Houses at L'Estaque* in Washington. Following a principle that Pissarro had already applied, the openings in the walls of houses, the doors and windows, are reduced in size, so that the walls are made as dense as possible and offer the maximum surface to light and shadow. But when Pissarro painted his houses this way, as early as 1867, in *Jallais Hill, Pontoise*, he was chiefly concerned with the problem of colour, volumes being less pronounced and extending over a single plane. With Cézanne, the problem was essentially one of construction. The planes of the ground and the rocks in *Houses at L'Estaque* are accentuated, but the geometric scheme he has in mind and his structural purpose are achieved through the direct and definite perception of this or that house, this or that piece of ground, this or that rock. The visual sensation is thus so thoroughly stripped to essentials, so much intensified, as to create an effect of primitivism. Comparing *Houses at L'Estaque* with the *Story of Joachim* in Giotto's Arena Chapel frescoes in Padua, one has the same revelation of the essential form of rocks and houses devoid of any ornament. The difference lies in the representation of light and shadow, which in Cézanne has become much more complex. Through light and shadow, through an ever more searching simplification, Cézanne distils the essence of things. The "theory" he applies is actually a critical method which excludes intellectualizing and allows free play to visual sensations in all their purity.

One result of this return to primitivism was his identification of the painting with the motif. It was between 1882 and 1887 that Cézanne created some of his most famous landscape motifs, like that of Mont Sainte-Victoire, the mountain dominating the landscape to the east of Aix, which he had painted from his youth and continued to paint all his life. Now he handled the theme with an unprecedented firmness and vitality. *Mont Sainte-Victoire, Environs of Gardanne* shows the unerring mastery he had gained over his regular volumes and their arrangement in space and depth. Houses and rocks are all treated with the same distribution of light and shadow, of pink and light blue tones beyond the green meadow, in order to build up the volumetric mass against the sky. Seen from Gardanne, the Sainte-Victoire is no more than a rocky ridge, and from the very bleakness of the motif Cézanne draws that simplicity and regularity which give forms their monumentality.

Camille Pissarro (1830–1903).
Jallais Hill, Pontoise, 1867. Oil. (34¹/4 x 45¹/4")
The Metropolitan Museum of Art, New York.
Bequest of William Church Osborn, 1951.

Houses at L'Estaque, 1880–1885. Oil. (25½ x 32″) Collection of Mr. and Mrs. Paul Mellon, National Gallery of Art, Washington, D.C.

Landscape, 1882–1886. Pencil. (19 1/4 x 13″)
Present whereabouts unknown.

View of L'Estaque, 1882–1885. Pencil. (17 5/16 x 10 1/4″)
Private Collection, Basel.

Mont Sainte-Victoire, Environs of Gardanne, 1885–1886. Oil. (24³/₄ x 36″) National Gallery of Art, Washington, D.C.

Seen from another point, from the village of Belle-vue, the mighty bulk of the mountain towers over the valley of the Arc; for example, in *Mont Sainte-Victoire with a Tall Pine*. But there Cézanne did not keep to the actual view; he brought the mountain closer in order to increase its volume and compensate for the deep hollow of the valley. He preferred his organized forms to the actual view, because they created a harmony and power which the actual view did not have. In the interests of that harmony, he treated the spatial recession as a surface pattern, this effect being emphasized by the tree framing the picture. Here the decorative intention is clear; but it is the decorative pattern assumed by any surface arrangement of pictorial elements, which does not necessarily eliminate an effect of depth and may

Mont Sainte-Victoire with Tall Pine, 1885–1887. Oil. (23¹/₂ x 28¹/₂") The Phillips Collection, Washington, D.C.

indeed make it all the sharper by contrast. How great are the force of representation and the emotional charge implicit in the decorative patterning of the *Mont Sainte-Victoire with a Tail Pine*, becomes clearer in the later versions of this theme painted by Cézanne in the 1890s.

Another favourite motif was the Gulf of Marseilles as seen from the town of L'Estaque. In the version in the Metropolitan Museum, New York, and in others, he had to cope with the same prob-lems of space as were raised by the Mont Sainte-Victoire.

In reality the mountains of Marseilleveyre are many miles away from L'Estaque, and can only be seen vaguely across the water. In order to indicate their structure, Cézanne brings them closer; but he preserves the spatial relation between near and far by moving back the foreground, which in reality was closer to him. Thus both foreground and background were shifted from their actual position,

Gulf of Marseilles Seen from L'Estaque, 1883–1885. Oil. (28³/4 x 39 1/2") The Metropolitan Museum of Art, New York. H.O. Havemeyer Collection.

and he excluded from the picture space the position which he had occupied himself, so doing away with any subjective reference. He treated the surface of the sea in the same way, painting it from a high enough angle to give it greater prominence and create the impression of a broader volume. In the Chicago version of the same subject, painted a few years later, the emphasis on the surface of the sea is still stronger, and the powerful volume of the mass of water, which is of course a colour mass, takes on an even more dramatic accent. And it is precisely this interposed mass of water that makes the background convincingly distant, even though the mountains have all the bulk of nearness. Cézanne thus organizes an objective relation between village, sea and mountains—objective not with respect to nature, but with respect to the picture, to art. In nature, "near" and "far" are material terms describing a finite world. Cézanne's work is so coherent, so self-contained, that it does not belong to any particular world; it forms a world of its own, partaking of the infinite and the universal and having the solemnity of everlasting things.

In this same period, in the 1880s, Cézanne painted some of his masterpieces on the theme of the Jas de Bouffan, his own house and estate about a mile outside Aix. It had inspired him as early as the 1860s; for example, the picture in the Tate Gallery, London. But it was only around 1885 that he succeeded in expressing through this theme the plastic force of empty space (Pushkin Museum, Moscow), the beauty and profusion of the leafage swaying in the wind (Courtauld Institute Galleries, London) and the spare grandeur of the trees when stripped of their leaves in winter (Minneapolis Institute of Arts). Thus in the grounds of the Jas de Bouffan, at every season of the year, Cézanne observed the life of nature and projected into it, through his art, the answering wealth of his own humanity.

Gulf of Marseilles Seen from L'Estaque,
1886–1890. Oil. (31 1/2 x 38 1/2")
Mr. and Mrs. Martin A. Ryerson Collection,
The Art Institute of Chicago.

Gulf of Marseilles Seen from L'Estaque (detail),
1886–1890. The Art Institute of Chicago. ▶

Chestnut Trees at the Jas de Bouffan, 1885–1887. Oil. (29 x 36⅝″) The Minneapolis Institute of Arts.
The William Hood Dunwoody Fund.

Chestnut Trees and Farm at the Jas de Bouffan, 1885–1887. Oil. (28³/4 x 36¹/4")
Pushkin Museum, Moscow.

102

Tall Trees at the Jas de Bouffan, 1885–1887. Oil. (25¹/₂ x 31¹/₄") Courtauld Institute Galleries, London.

The Alley of Chestnut Trees at the Jas de Bouffan, 1884–1887. Pencil. (12¹/₁₆ x 18¹³/₁₆")
Boymans-van Beuningen Museum, Rotterdam.

Landscape, 1884–1887. Pencil. (13³/₄ x 21¹/₄") Reproduced by courtesy of the Trustees of the British Museum, London.

1

1. *Landscape with Poplar Tree, 1873–1876.*
   Pencil. (11⁷/₁₆ x 6¹/₂″)
   Present whereabouts unknown.

2. *Study of Trees, 1886–1889. Pencil.*
   (14⁹/₁₆ x 18⁷/₈″) Present whereabouts
   unknown.

3. *Study of Trees, 1884–1887. Pencil.*
   (11¹³/₁₆ x 18¹/₈″) Collection
   Perry T. Rathbone, Cambridge,
   Massachusetts.

4. *Landscape with Houses, c. 1885.*
   Pencil. Measurements not recorded.
   Present whereabouts unknown.

5. *View of Gardanne, 1885–1886.*
   Pencil. (8¹/₄ x 12″)
   The Museum of Modern Art, New York.
   Lillie P. Bliss Collection.

6. *Sloping Trees, 1896–1899.*
   Pencil. (12 x 18¹/₂″)
   Collection A. Deuber, Basel.

7. *Study of Trees, 1896–1899.*
   Pencil. (18¹/₂ x 12³/₁₆″)
   Present whereabouts unknown.

3

4

5

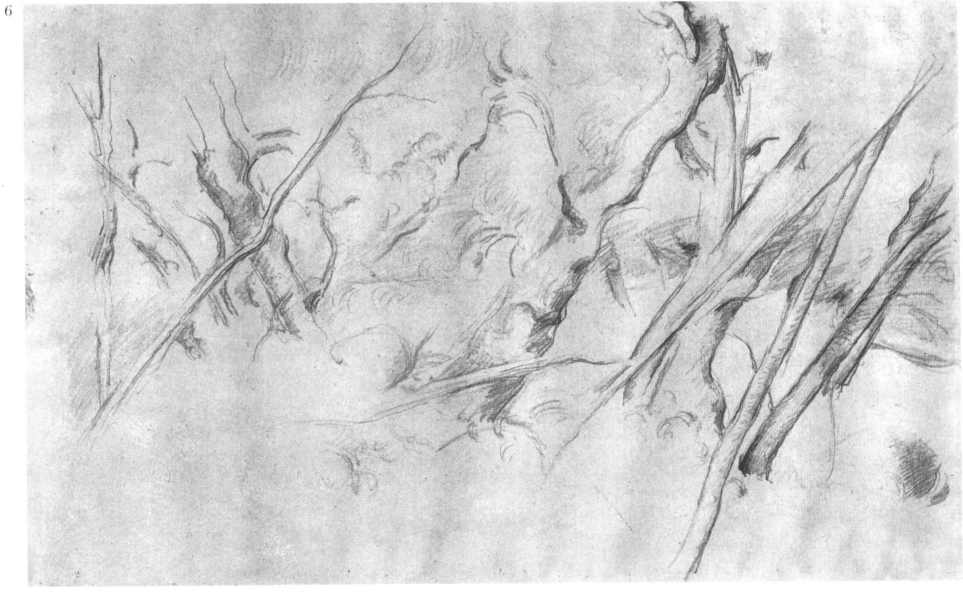

6

The Blue Vase, 1885–1887. Oil. (24 x 19⅝″) Galerie du Jeu de Paume, Louvre, Paris.

Self-Portrait with Palette and Easel, 1885–1887. Oil. (36¹/4 x 28³/4″) Stiftung Sammlung E.G. Bührle, Zürich.

Vase of Flowers and Two Apples, 1883–1887. Oil. (21⅝ x 18⅛") Private Collection, Paris.

It was not only the Provençal landscape that called forth his deepest response: whatever the theme he chose, a still life, a vase of flowers, a portrait, he infused it with the same sense of the everlasting and the monumental, without ornament or rhetoric. The *Vase of Flowers and Two Apples* (Private Collection, Paris) is a good example. The colours, though simplified, are very intense. The foreground plane is tipped up sharply to stress the volumes of vase and apples; yet the volumes do not overweight the composition, whose dense weave of contrasting colour planes creates a compact, organic space. In the *Portrait of Madame Cézanne* (Philadelphia) the strongly marked volumes are nevertheless handled with lightness and grace. Cézanne by now was a master of pictorial construction, and after 1887 he was able to give a freer rein to his imagination and achieve a more effective synthesis of form. Not only the structure but the whole picture space became vibrant with impassioned feeling: landscapes, objects and human figures were transmuted into a new geometric and emotional order of painting.

Madame Cézanne Dozing, c. 1885.
Pencil. (12 x 9 1/4")
Present whereabouts unknown.

The Artist's Son Paul Writing, c. 1885.
Pencil. (8 7/8 x 12 3/16")
Present whereabouts unknown.

Portrait of Madame Cézanne, 1885. Oil. (15¼ x 19″) Philadelphia Museum of Art.

Bridge over the Marne at Créteil, 1888. Oil. (28 x 35¹/₂") Pushkin Museum, Moscow.

*Self-Portrait with Bowler Hat, 1883–1887. Oil.
(17¹/₂ x 14″) Ny Carlsberg Glyptotek, Copenhagen.*

6

The Art Theories
of Cézanne

BEFORE describing Cézanne's work in the
last sixteen years of his life, I should like to
pause for a moment and consider his ideas
about art.

Cézanne never departed from the visual sensations aroused in him by nature, even though he
rendered them in an ever more abstract manner:
he was aware, moreover, that "an era of new art is
in the making."[1] This evolution of his art was a
spontaneous growth; it was not something deliberate or contrived. It was as if he hit on his abstract
forms each time he tackled a painting and was
struck with surprise at his own discoveries. In the
1880s he succeeded in imposing his indefinable
order on his sensations, and from that order they
drew their force and clarity. Witness a painting of

1888, the *Bridge over the Marne at Créteil*. Here he
develops space in depth and accentuates the synthetic character to obtain an effect of monumentality. A perfect balance is achieved between voids
(the sky and the part of the water free of reflections)
and solids, the latter including the reflections in the
water which, while given their necessary trans-
parency, have nevertheless the density of solid volumes. For all the variety of yellows, reds and greens,
the colours fit into an overall harmony of contrasts
and gradations of blue. The unity of vision within
a rich variety of elements is perfectly achieved—
absolute in its firmness, sureness and grandeur.

In the *Still Life with Basket of Fruit (The Kitchen
Table)*, as Erle Loran has shown, the basket of fruit
stands on a different level from the actual plane of

115

the table, and the left side of the table extending beyond the cloth is out of true with the right side. In other words, Cézanne deliberately distorted objects in order to represent them from different angles, to turn round them and bring out the fullness of their volumes, and to convey by the liberties he took the vital energy of objects. The beauty of his still lifes, acknowledged by all who see them, depends precisely on the commanding authority with which he convinces us that his "distorted" vision is truer and more vital than our own.

It is therefore all the more interesting to consider Cézanne's position in the last two decades of the nineteenth century and his unrivalled contribution to the later development of art. Obviously he keeps to visual appearances, and meant to keep to them, however much he adapts or reorders them in accordance with a sensory and spiritual response. In this his painting differs radically from that of the Cubists a few years later. But it is obvious too that the principles of Cubism are to be found in Cézanne. From 1904 dates his famous letter to Emile Bernard: "Treat nature in terms of the cylinder, the sphere and the cone, the whole being put into perspective, so that each side of an object and a plane is directed towards a central point. The lines parallel to the

Still Life "Pain sans mie," 1887–1890. Pencil. (12 x 19 1/2") Collection Lord Clark, London.

Still Life with Basket of Fruit (The Kitchen Table), c. 1888–1890. Oil. (25⅝ x 31⅞″) *Galerie du Jeu de Paume, Louvre, Paris.*

117

horizon give breadth, whether it is a section of nature or, if you prefer, of the spectacle which the Pater Omnipotens Aeterne Deus displays before our eyes. The lines perpendicular to this horizon give depth. But nature for us men is more depth than surface. Hence the necessity of introducing into our vibrations of light, represented by reds and yellows, a sufficient amount of bluish tones in order to give the feeling of air."[2]

As to cylinders, spheres and cones, none are to be seen in Cézanne's pictures. This phrase, then, may be taken to express an ideal aspiration towards an organization of forms transcending nature, and nothing more. The same is true of other sayings of his: "The method emerges from contact with nature. It develops according to circumstances. It consists in searching for the expression of what one feels and in organizing one's sensation in a personal aesthetic."[3] Or again, as recorded by Emile Bernard: "The transposition made by the painter, in an outlook of his own, gives a new interest to nature as he reproduces it. He writes in painting what has not yet been painted. He makes it into painting absolutely; that is, something other than reality. This is no longer a matter of flat imitation."[4]

Many years later, in 1923, Juan Gris wrote: "The mathematics of painting are leading me to representational physics." A notion which seems similar to that of Cézanne. The difference is revealed when Gris plainly states: "The world from which I draw the elements of reality is not visual but imaginative."[5]

Cézanne's is still very much a visual and sensorial world, whose validity he recognized through his experience of Impressionism, and even in these later years he said that he wanted to make of Impressionism "something solid and enduring like the art of the museums." If in his painting he anticipates certain features which later, with different results, entered into Cubism, it is because he steadily aimed at an ever more thorough synthesis between emotion and form, or rather between emotion and space. So it is that, as in *The Kitchen Table*, he breaks away from the traditional perspective representation and sets up different perspectives from several viewpoints; that is, he identifies space with a visual sequence of images which, reacting on the mind, create that identity of space and time which Bergson, at about the same period, called "real duration."

All this Cézanne did without any preconceived theories and, needless to say, without having read Bergson. He carried out his analysis of space according to the principle of duration in order to infuse objects, seen from more than one point of view, with an intensity and vitality never achieved before—this, then, through an analysis of space which also involved a synthesis of vision.

It was done not in an abstract order of the mind, but on the concrete plane of visual sensations to which he always held fast. The multiple perspective served to intensify the sensation which, far from being a thing external or superficial, entailed a searching analysis of the motif. "Sensation, with Cézanne, is at the bottom of all his work. All the rest is only the skeleton. He always goes to nature for his forms."[6] But primacy of sensation did not mean disregard of pictorial and compositional order. A Cézanne painting is always the product of a rigorous organization of forms, and so tended increasingly towards abstraction and away from realistic imitation.

In the 1870s he had found in Impressionism a corrective to the second-hand realism which he had brought with him to Paris from Provence. When he parted company with his impressionist friends, it was to pursue a path of his own in the direction of abstraction.

A letter of 25 January 1904, addressed to Louis Aurenche,[7] throws light on the process that carried him from the sensation of nature to style: "You speak to me in your letter of my realization in art. I believe I am achieving it more each day, though rather laboriously. For while the strong sensation of nature—and with me certainly it is keen—is the necessary basis of any conception of art, and on it repose the grandeur and beauty of the work to be, the knowledge of the means of expressing our emotion is no less essential, and can only be acquired by very long experience." Clearly, for him, that "very long experience" was the means by which he worked out his own style through the practice of painting. In the last years of his life he was well aware that the confrontation with visual appearances was not enough to express his sensation, that in addition to it he required an abstract means—style. Through style, even if it meant sacrificing visual appearances, he was able to transform his sensation into emotion and make it vital and lasting thanks to the resources of his art.

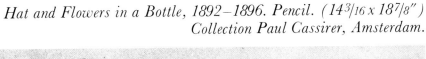

Hat and Flowers in a Bottle, 1892–1896. Pencil. (14³/16 x 18⁷/8″)
Collection Paul Cassirer, Amsterdam.

Self-Portrait, 1890–1894. Oil. (18¹/₈ x 15³/₄″) Private Collection, Paris.

Self-Portrait, 1880–1882. Pencil. (8⁵/₈ x 4⁷/₈")
Private Collection, New York.

7

Passion and Grandeur

DURING the years from 1882 to 1888 Cézanne seemed to find in landscape the subject that best enabled him to order and clarify his sensations. From 1890 till the end of the century, his masterpieces are for the most part figure paintings.

The *Self-Portrait* of 1890–1894 (Private Collection, Paris) is perhaps the most poignantly human likeness of himself that he ever gave us. The interlocking of the facial planes is as forceful here as it is in the rocky slopes of *Mont Sainte-Victoire, Environs of Gardanne* (Washington); yet the facial expression, the man's good nature, his keen and penetrating glance, are tellingly conveyed. The volumes of head and bust are perfectly framed in space, standing out with powerful immediacy.

To the figure of *Madame Cézanne in the Conservatory*, placed in the open air, he gives an expression of grace, freedom and natural dignity. The unbroken line of the brow, the oval of the face set off by the dark hair-line, the formal regularity of nose, mouth and chin, all tell of the artist's geometric ideal. But that ideal gains life from the delicacy of the tones, of the flesh-tints lit up by gleams of yellow, pink and red and shadowed over with green and blue. It is colour that gives serenity, grace and the breath of life to this face, which rises like a flower over the blue of the dress, over the touches of red, green and yellow in the background. This picture is a typical instance of an "unfinished" Cézanne, the lack of finish being not a failure of realization but on the contrary a refinement of realization.

XXXVII

Self-Portrait, c. 1883. Pencil. (8⁹/₁₆ x 4⁷/₈″)
The Art Institute of Chicago.

Full-Length Study of the Artist's Son Paul, c. 1885. Pencil.
(19¹/₄ x 12³/₁₆″)
The A.L. Hillman Family Foundation, New York.

Madame Cézanne in the Conservatory, c. 1890. Oil. (36¼ x 28¾″) The Metropolitan Museum of Art, New York.

The Card Players, 1890–1892. Oil. (38 1/8 x 51 1/4") Private Collection, Paris.

A tower-like solidity is impressed upon the *Woman with a Coffee Pot*, seen frontally with unsparing directness. The position of the figure in space and the stark prominence of the setting give its sturdy unity to the picture. The intense blue of the dress, faceted round the volume of the body, that is to say built up with light, contrasts with the delicate pinkish-grey of the panelling and the orange flesh-tints.

Among Cézanne's finest works is the series of *Card Players*. Again and again he returned to this theme, varying the number of players, but perhaps the most fully realized of all is the version of 1890–1892 (Pri-

Woman with a Coffee Pot, 1890–1894. Oil. (51³/₈ x 38″) Galerie du Jeu de Paume, Louvre, Paris.

vate Collection, Paris). The colour scheme hinges on the contrast between the purplish-blue coat of the lefthand player and the blue-shaded yellow of the righthand player, and on that between these tones and the reds of background and flesh and the yellow of the table. From the infinite gradations of these colours arise the volumes of figures and things. Their firmness, the well-defined action of the players, and the solid unity of the composition show that the intensity of the colours has not riven but cemented the whole. Continuous outlines would have isolated the figures; instead, they hold together because, like the table and the background, they are built up with zones of colour. By means of this rhythmic composition of colour zones, he substitutes modulation for modelling. The closely knit design of the picture springs from the flawless tissue of interrelated planes.

In a letter to Léo Larguier he wrote: "Painting is not a matter of copying the object slavishly; it is a matter of discerning a harmony between many relations." And the unity arising from these relations is not physical but spiritual. Instead of giving us the physical frame, he gives us the character of the two peasants playing cards. "Seeing from nature," he said, "means bringing out the character of one's model." A peasant by Cézanne is individualized like a portrait, universalized like an idea; he is as solemn as a monument, as firm as a moral conscience. To Jules Borély, he said: "Above all things I like the look of people who have grown old without doing violence to custom, surrendering to the laws of the time. Look at that old café proprietor seated before his doorway, what style he has!" Cézanne found nobility of style not in conventions but in the sincerity of unvarnished reality, in life lived in the spirit of truth. Thanks to that sincerity and truthfulness, each of these figures stands before us, not as a card player reflecting a casual or momentary interval of

the game, but as a self-contained existence arrested by art and fixed for eternity. Artistic sensitivity, scrupulous workmanship and moral rigour go to create a new beauty, among the most majestic and solemn in the history of art.

*Coat on a Chair, 1890–1900. Watercolour and pencil. (18 x 18¼")
Collection Marianne Feilchenfeldt, Zürich.*

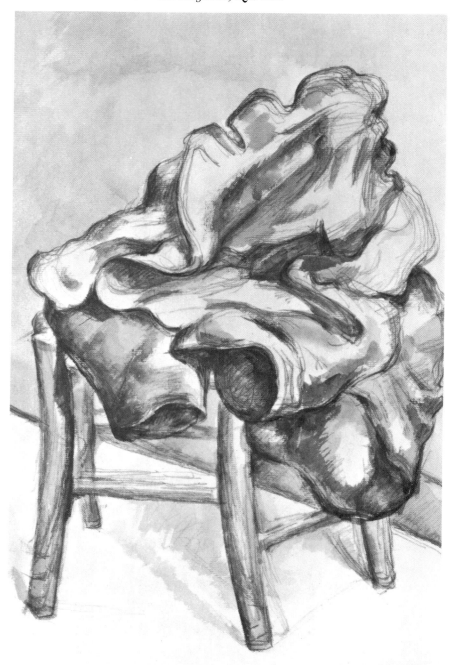

Card Player, 1890–1892. Watercolour and pencil.
(14¹/₄ x 19¹/₈″) The Art Institute of Chicago.

Card Player, 1895–1900. Watercolour and pencil. (19¹/₈ x 14³/₈″)
Estate of Baron von Hirsch.

Card Player, 1890–1892. Watercolour and pencil. (19¹/₁₆ x 14¹/₄″)
Museum of Art, Rhode Island School of Design, Providence.

127

Boy in a Red Waistcoat, 1890–1895. Oil. (31¹/₂ x 25³/₈") Stiftung Sammlung E.G. Bührle, Zürich.

An exceptional grace emanates from the series of portraits of a young Italian model, dressed as a peasant of the Roman Campagna and known as *The Boy in a Red Waistcoat*. The version in the Museum of Modern Art, New York, is the most vital, the one in the Mellon Collection the most elegant, the one in the Bührle Foundation, Zürich, the most painterly. In all three the harmony is perfectly realized, despite the intensity of the colours. Early critics were scandalized by the excessive length of the right arm in the Bührle version. But this distortion gives the picture its ideal and expressive proportions, and underpins the majestic tranquillity of the pose.

Studies for "Mardi Gras," c. 1888. Pencil. (7¹/₄ x 9³/₄") Kunstmuseum, Basel.

Boy in a Red Waistcoat (detail), 1890–1895.
Stiftung Sammlung E.G. Bührle, Zürich. ▶

The Struggle of Love, 1875–1876. Oil. (16¹/₂ x 21⁵/₈")
Private Collection, Paris.

In 1895 Cézanne painted the portrait of his friend, the writer and critic Gustave Geffroy. The architectonic value of the figure in relation to the setting is fully realized, and the whole picture has an even more monumental solidity than *The Card Players*. The blue of the coat and the purplish red of the chair stand out powerfully against the yellow volumes on the bookshelves.

Again and again, in the course of his long career, Cézanne painted pictures of bathers, both men and women. It was this theme that, in younger years, enabled him to emancipate himself from romantic subjects; and by composing nude figures in the open air, in relation to daylight, and modulating the tones in the same way for figures, trees and water, he learned to give unity to the picture. Over the years he painted many masterpieces on the theme of

Sheet of Studies with Bathers, 1872–1876. Pencil. (7⁷/₈ x 11³/₁₆") Present whereabouts unknown.

Three Women Bathers, 1879–1882. Oil. (22⁷/₈ x 21¹/₂″)
Musée du Petit Palais, Paris.

Large Bathers, 1900–1905. Oil. (52³/₈ x 81¹/₂″) © The Barnes Foundation, Merion, Pa.

133

Large Bathers, 1898–1905. Oil. (82 x 99″) Philadelphia Museum of Art: Purchased: The W.P. Wilstach Collection.

bathers. Among the most famous are *The Struggle of Love* (Private Collection, Paris) and *Bathers at Rest* (Barnes Foundation, Merion, Pa.), both of the 1870s. But the grandest of all are the bathers painted in the last years of his life, both in oils and water-colours. Orange yellow is the chief tone of light, and violet-blue-green that of shadow: this contrast accentuates the overall colour harmony. At the end of his life he painted several versions of the so-called *Large Bathers*. The one in the Philadelphia Museum is the most architectonic. The figure group fits into an ideal pyramid formed by the trees and the lateral figures: the effect is as solemn and monumental as a cathedral façade. The version in the Barnes Foundation is more dramatic: the branches, with lights and shadows contending among them, shoot out like arrows and break off sharply. Ever present in his *Bathers*, both large and small, is a monumental design that acts as a necessary check on the dramatic impetus.

Bathers, 1895–1900. Watercolour. (7¹/₈ x 9⁷/₈″) Present whereabouts unknown.

Portrait of Vallier, 1904–1906. Oil. (25⁵/₈ x 21¹/₂″) Stiftung Sammlung E.G. Bührle, Zürich.

When, in the last years, he painted the series of portraits of his gardener Vallier, the dramatic expression becomes more intense and flows unchecked: these pictures are dialogues with death, poignant in their profound and tragic accents. Some of them are watercolours, some are oils, usually painted with a full brush, so that the figure stands firm, four-square, insistent. The old gardener is seen with so moved and moving a sympathy that, through him, we sense the personality of Cézanne himself, at the very end of his life, as if he were painting a moral self-portrait at one remove. Such, one feels, was Cézanne himself at grips with his daily task: stoic, intent, nursing no hopes, but strong in the conviction of accomplishing his appointed task.

1. *Mercury Fastening his Heel Wings,*
   after Pigalle, 1873–1876. Pencil.
   (16¹/8 x 10⁵/8″)
   Present whereabouts unknown.

2. *Atlas, after Pierre Puget, 1874–1877.*
   Pencil. (11⁷/16 x 9¹/4″)
   Private Collection, Zürich.

3. *Study after Bellona in Rubens'*
   "Apotheosis of Henry IV," 1879–1882.
   Pencil. (17³/4 x 10¹/4″)
   Estate of Baron von Hirsch.

4. *The Venus of Milo, 1880–1883.*
   Pencil. (18¹¹/16 x 11″)
   Formerly Collection Jacques Lipchitz,
   Hastings-on-Hudson, New York.

5. *A Slave, after Michelangelo, 1885–1888.*
   Pencil. (17⁵/8 x 11⁵/8″)
   Detroit Institute of Arts.

6. *Crouching Venus, after C.-A. Coysevox,*
   1885–1888. Pencil. (18¹/2 x 11¹³/16″)
   Collection Mrs. Kasser, New York.

7. *Milo of Crotona, after Pierre Puget, c. 1890.*
   Pencil. (25¹/8 x 12³/8″) Baltimore Museum
   of Art, Frederic W. Cone Bequest.

8. *Hercules Resting, after Pierre Puget,*
   1887–1890. Pencil. (19¹/4 x 12³/8″)
   Present whereabouts unknown.

9. *Hercules Resting, after Pierre Puget,*
   1884–1887. Pencil. (18¹/2 x 11¹³/16″)
   Present whereabouts unknown.

10. *Study after The Flayed Man ("L'Ecorché"),*
    1893–1896. Pencil.
    (8¹/4 x 5⁵/16″) Private Collection, Paris.

11. *Pierre Mignard, after Desjardins, 1892–1895.*
    Pencil. (8¹/16 x 4⁷/8″) Kunstmuseum, Basel.

12. *Study after the Cupid attributed to Puget,*
    1886–1889. Pencil. (11⁵/8 x 9¹/16″)
    Formerly Kunsthalle, Bremen (lost during
    World War II).

13. *Study after the Cupid attributed to Puget,*
    1886–1889. Pencil. (19¹/2 x 11¹³/16″)
    Private Collection, Cambridge, Mass.

14. *Study after the Cupid attributed to Puget,*
    1879–1882. Pencil. (18¹/2 x 15″) Collection
    Carl Roesch, Diessenhofen, Switzerland.

1

2

3

4

5

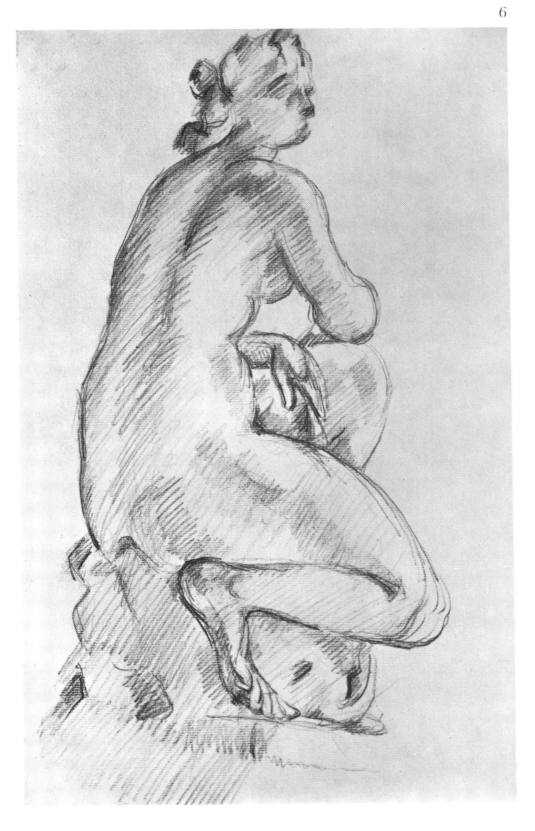

6

7

141

8

9

10

Cézanne, Paul.   1935.137.

12

13

14

His ability to convey the impulses of his spirit as if they were those of nature gave the mature Cézanne a wonderful freedom and power over the subject. A few apples on a table (Museum of Modern Art, New York) become in his hands a tragedy of unfathomable implications. So radical is the transmutation of fruit, glass and pitcher into light and shadow, into violet blue, reds and orange yellows that one is borne beyond the objects in a surge of passion that sweeps over the colours and saturates them with intense and turbulent life.

This is not an isolated example. The joy had gone out of his soul. The luxuriant richness that he had impressed on his earlier still lifes has disappeared, even when heavy hangings are added to vary the motifs. In place of that richness, of the old pleasure in sheer physical beauty, are depth upon depth of dramatic passion.

Still Life with Apples and Pitcher, 1895–1898. Oil. (27 x 36¹/2″) The Museum of Modern Art, New York. Lillie P. Bliss Collection.

Still Life with Plaster Cupid, c. 1895. Oil. (27¹/₂ x 22¹/₂″) Courtauld Institute Galleries, London.

Mont Sainte-Victoire, 1904–1906. Oil. (27⁷/₈ x 36¹/₈″) Philadelphia Museum of Art:
Purchased: The George W. Elkins Collection.

Self-Portrait, 1897–1900. Pencil. (12³/₁₆ x 9⁷/₁₆″)
Estate of Baron von Hirsch.

A Cosmic Harmony

APICTURE of *Mont Sainte-Victoire* (V. 665, present whereabouts unknown), painted between 1895 and 1900, shows what energy of representation, what depth of emotion, the artist found in nature and in the apparently decorative transformation of the natural motif. Here the mountain no longer closes off the broad valley: dominating the composition, its mighty bulk becomes almost menacing. The rocky mass is brought closer by the sketchiness of the foreground, and the simplified forms of the rocks have the controlled tension of arrested movement. Again passion prevails over contemplation: the serene vision of the broad valley gives way to the cry of the pent-up forces of earth.

In 1896, during a short stay in Savoy, he painted *The Lake of Annecy* from the lakeside village of Tal-loires. The unity of vision is so complete that the lake waters throb with the same pulse as trees, houses and mountains, everything being fused with the blue that enters into the lights and shadows and shades off into pink and green. A panic sense of overwhelming grandeur informs the order of nature as here recreated by art.

As he grew older, the sense of style that carried him towards the monumental was accompanied by a deepening earnestness reflecting his tragic sense of life. In *The Maison Maria* of 1895–1898 (Private Collection), an old house full of cracks in the Aix countryside, one has intimations of the upheaval that had shaken the artist's own soul; and that dramatic tension recurs in the many pictures of another old building near by, known as the Château

Noir, where he rented a room from 1895 to 1899, and also in the pictures of the Bibémus quarry in the same neighbourhood to the east of Aix.

In the earlier versions of *The Quarry of Bibémus* (the one in the Folkwang Museum, Essen, for example), he emphasizes the sharp cut of the rocks, the plastic energy of their squared, geometrical forms, even when, as in some of them (Baltimore Museum, for example), the Mont Sainte-Victoire looms up beyond in all its majesty. The colour here is intense, but its force is lessened by the broken pattern of the rocks. Later, especially after 1900, the colour tones become more impassioned, and the Château Noir (actually built of fine yellow stone from the Bibémus quarry) looms up amid darker colours like a magic glow of light; or again, as in a late version in London (Private Collection), it is shrouded in the mysterious shades of evening.

The Château Noir, 1895–1900. Watercolour and pencil. (14¹/₈ x 20³/₄") Boymans-van Beuningen Museum, Rotterdam.

The Lake of Annecy, 1896. Oil. (25½ x 32″) Courtauld Institute Galleries, London.

The Maison Maria on the Road to the Château Noir, 1895–1898. Oil. (25⁵/₈ x 31⁷/₈″) Private Collection.

View of the Château Noir, 1894–1896. Oil. (28³/4 x 36¹/4″) Collection Oskar Reinhart am Römerholz, Winterthur, Switzerland.

The Quarry of Bibémus, 1898–1900. Oil. (25⅝ x 31⅞″) Folkwang Museum, Essen.

Then harmony prevailed over the surge of passion, a cosmic harmony achieved and maintained in a final series of views of Mont Sainte-Victoire. Cézanne seemed to look upon the mountain again with something of the fresh and candid eye of youth, but also with the collected detachment and resignation of a lifetime's experience. He saw it at a farther remove than before, like a spiritual apparition beyond an immense gulf of space, like a heavenward aspiration.

The landmarks in Cézanne's development stand out clearly: the achieving of a personal style, romantic, introspective and turbulent, around 1865; the experience of Impressionism beginning in 1872; the focusing of his powers on the construction of the picture from 1878 on; and then a growing freedom towards construction, towards nature, towards his own theory of art, as in the end he spontaneously created a monumental, architectonic harmony, wrought out of his own sensations, his own passion. Of all the conflicts at work in the mind and soul of this artist, the counterbalancing demands of monumentality and passion were certainly the most fruitful, both artistically and spiritually. Without the earlier experiences, the final harmony would not have been possible. But the exultation that quickens the impressionist and constructive paintings has gone from the late works. The organ notes of the latter are too solemn for gladness. But their humanity is deeper, and the dedication of every brushstroke is so urgent and entire that all meaning and existence in the world seems to be concentrated in this painting. Beyond Cézanne's masterpieces, beyond his own life, glows his steadfast faith in painting.

Study of a Tree, 1895–1900. Watercolour. (10⁷/₈ x 17¹/₈″) Kunsthaus, Zürich.

Mont Sainte-Victoire, c. 1900. Watercolour. (12¹/₄ x 18⁷/₈″) Cabinet des Dessins, Louvre, Paris.

Mont Sainte-Victoire, 1904–1906. Oil. (23⁵/8 x 28³/4″) Kunstmuseum, Basel.

◄ *Mont Sainte-Victoire (detail), 1904–1906. Oil. Kunstmuseum, Basel.*

Cézanne in his studio at Les Lauves, Aix, in front of his "Large Bathers." Photograph taken by Emile Bernard in 1904.

Notes

1. Cézanne and Contemporary Criticism

[1] John Rewald, *Cézanne, sa vie, son œuvre, son amitié pour Zola*, Paris 1939, p. 24.

[2] John Rewald, op. cit., p. 30.

[3] John Rewald, op. cit., p. 95.

[4] John Rewald, op. cit., p. 105.

[5] John Rewald, op. cit., p. 107.

[6] John Rewald, op. cit., p. 107.

[7] Paul Cézanne, *Correspondance*, edited by John Rewald, Paris 1937, p. 94.

[8] Alfred H. Barr, Jr., "Cézanne d'après les lettres de Marion à Morstatt," *Gazette des Beaux-Arts*, Paris, January 1937, p. 37.

[9] Emile Zola, *Mon Salon*, Paris 1866, reprinted in *Mes Haines*, Paris 1866.

[10] John Rewald, *Cézanne, sa vie, son œuvre, son amitié pour Zola*, Paris 1939, pp. 129–130.

[11] John Rewald, op. cit., p. 131.

[12] Alfred H. Barr, Jr., op. cit.

[13] John Rewald, op. cit., p. 140.

[14] John Rewald, op. cit., p. 149.

[15] John Rewald, op. cit., p. 150.

[16] John Rewald, op. cit., p. 152.

[17] Emile Zola, "Le naturalisme au Salon," *Le Voltaire*, Paris, 18–22 June 1880. Reprinted in F.W.J. Hemmings and Robert J. Niess, *Emile Zola: Salons*, Geneva-Paris 1959.

[18] John Rewald, *The History of Impressionism*, 2nd edition, Museum of Modern Art, New York 1961, p. 534.

[19] John Rewald, *Cézanne, sa vie, son œuvre, son amitié pour Zola*, Paris 1939, p. 168.

[20] Paul Cézanne, *Correspondance*, Paris 1937, pp. 98–99.

[21] John Rewald, op. cit., p. 196.

[22] John Rewald, op. cit., pp. 202–203.

[23] Paul Cézanne, *Correspondance*, Paris 1937, pp. 122–123.

[24] Georges Rivière, in *L'Impressionniste, Journal d'Art*, Paris, 6–28 April 1877. Reprinted in Lionello Venturi, *Les Archives de l'Impressionnisme*, Durand-Ruel, Paris-New York 1939, vol. II, pp. 308–323.

[25] John Rewald, op. cit., pp. 260–261.

[26] Letter to Octave Maus of 27 November 1889, in Paul Cézanne, *Correspondance*, Paris 1937, p. 214.

[27] John Rewald, op. cit., p. 103.

[28] John Rewald, op. cit., p. 164.

[29] Joris-Karl Huysmans, *Certains*, Paris 1889. The reference here is to the 4th edition, Paris 1904, pp. 42–43.

[30] Gustave Geffroy, *Histoire de l'Impressionnisme*, La vie artistique, 3e série, Paris 1894, p. 248 ff.

[31] Letter to Gustave Geffroy of 26 March 1894, in Paul Cézanne, *Correspondance*, Paris 1937, p. 216.

[32] Paul Cézanne, op. cit., pp. 237–238.

[33] From Alfred de Vigny's poem "Moïse," published 1822–1823: "Lord, you made me mighty and solitary, Let me sleep the sleep of the earth."

[34] Gustave Geffroy, *La Peinture en France de 1850 à 1900*, La vie artistique, 6e série, Paris 1900, pp. 219–220.

[35] Thadée Natanson, "Paul Cézanne," *La Revue Blanche*, Paris, IX, 2e semestre, 1895, pp. 496–500. Reprinted in Natanson's *Claude Monet et Paul Cézanne*, Paris 1900.

[36] André Mellerio, *Le mouvement idéaliste en peinture*, Paris 1896, p. 18.

[37] Vincent van Gogh, Letter 613 to Theo, in *The Complete Letters of Vincent van Gogh*, 3 vols., London and New York 1958, vol. 3, p. 227.

[38] Félicien Fagus, "Quarante tableaux de Cézanne," *La Revue Blanche*, Paris, XX, September-December 1899, pp. 627–628.

[39] Emile Bernard, "Paul Cézanne," *L'Occident*, Paris, July 1904, pp. 17–30.

[40] Charles Morice (editor), "Enquête sur les tendances actuelles des arts plastiques," *Mercure de France*, Paris, LVI, No. 195, 1 August 1905, p. 346 ff. The survey was continued in the issues of 15 August and 1 September 1905.

[41] Maurice Denis, "Cézanne," *L'Occident*, Paris, September 1907. Reprinted in Denis's *Théories, 1890–1910*, Paris 1912.

[42] Ardengo Soffici's Cézanne essay of 1908 was reprinted in his *Scoperte e massacri*, Vallecchi, Florence 1919.

[43] Jacques Rivière, *Etudes*, N.R.F., Paris 1910, p. 41 ff.

[44] *Cézanne*, Bernheim-Jeune, Paris 1914, with texts by Octave Mirbeau, Théodore Duret, Léon Werth and Francis Jourdain, and letters from Cézanne to Gaston Bernheim-Jeune (de Villers).

[45] Ambroise Vollard, *Paul Cézanne*, Paris 1914. English translation: *Paul Cézanne, His Life and Art*, New York 1923.

2. Cézanne Criticism After 1920

[1] Simon Lévy's letter is printed in André Salmon, *Propos d'atelier*, Paris 1922, p. 99.

[2] C.F. Ramuz, *L'exemple de Cézanne, suivi de Pages sur Cézanne*, Lausanne 1951.

[3] Joachim Gasquet, *Cézanne*, Paris 1921; 2nd edition, Paris 1926.

[4] Roger Fry, *Cézanne, A Study of His Development*, London and New York 1927.

[5] Henri Focillon, *La Peinture aux XIXe et XXe siècles*, Paris 1928, vol. II, pp. 270–300.

[6] Giorgio Castelfranco, *La Pittura moderna*, Florence 1934, pp. 42–43.

[7] Eugenio d'Ors, *Paul Cézanne*, Paris 1930 and London 1936.

[8] Lionello Venturi, *Cézanne, son art, son œuvre*, 2 volumes (text and plates), Paul Rosenberg, Paris 1936.

[9] Gerstle Mack, *Paul Cézanne*, New York and London 1935.

[10] Paul Cézanne, *Correspondance*, edited by John Rewald, Paris 1937. English edition: Paul Cézanne, *Letters*, London 1941.

[11] John Rewald, *Cézanne, sa vie, son œuvre, son amitié pour Zola*, Paris 1939. English version: *Paul Cézanne*, New York 1948.

[12] Fritz Novotny, *Paul Cézanne*, Vienna 1937.

[13] Bernard Dorival, *Paul Cézanne*, Paris 1948.

[14] Liliane Guerry, *Cézanne et l'expression de l'espace*, Paris 1950.

[15] Pierre Francastel, *Peinture et société*, Paris 1951.

[16] Meyer Schapiro, *Paul Cézanne*, New York and London 1952.

[17] Lawrence Gowing, catalogue introduction for the exhibition *Cézanne Paintings*, Edinburgh and London, Tate Gallery, summer-autumn, 1954.

[18] Kurt Badt, *Die Kunst Cézannes*, Munich 1956. English translation: *The Art of Cézanne*, University of California Press, Berkeley and Los Angeles 1965.

[19] Gertrude Berthold, *Cézanne und die alten Meister*, Stuttgart 1958.

3. Cézanne as a Romantic

[1] Joachim Gasquet, *Cézanne*, Paris 1921. The reference here is to the 2nd edition, Paris 1926, p. 180.

4. Impressionism

[1] "Vivifier Poussin sur nature": quoted from Cézanne by Charles Camoin in his answer to the "Enquête sur les tendances actuelles des arts plastiques," *Mercure de France*, Paris, 1 August, 15 August, 1 September 1905.

[2] Letter to Octave Maus of 27 November 1889, in Paul Cézanne, *Correspondance*, Paris 1937, p. 214.

[3] Letter to Marius Roux, in Paul Cézanne, *Correspondance*, Paris 1937.

6. The Art Theories of Cézanne

[1] Letter to Charles Camoin of 28 January 1902, in Paul Cézanne, *Correspondance*, Paris 1937, p. 245.

[2] Letter to Emile Bernard of 15 April 1904, ibid., p. 259.

[3] John Rewald, *Cézanne, sa vie, son œuvre, son amitié pour Zola*, Paris 1939, p. 348.

[4] Emile Bernard, *Souvenirs sur Paul Cézanne*, Paris 1921, p. 273.

[5] D.H. Kahnweiler, *Juan Gris*, Paris 1946, p. 272.

[6] Simon Lévy, *Cézanne*, Paris 1933.

[7] Paul Cézanne, *Correspondance*, Paris 1937, p. 257.

Biographical Outline and Contemporary Events

1839 Birth of Paul Cézanne on 19 January at 28 Rue de l'Opéra in Aix-en-Provence, where his father Louis-Auguste Cézanne was a prosperous hatter, specializing in the sale and export of felt hats. The Cézanne family, though originating from the small town of Cesana in Piedmont, on the Italian side of the Mont Genèvre, was of French stock. Paul's birth was followed by that of two sisters, Marie (1841) and Rose (1854).

- 1839 Birth of Alfred Sisley (1839–1899).
  Stendhal publishes *La Chartreuse de Parme*.
- 1840 Birth of Claude Monet (1840–1926).
- 1841 Birth of Auguste Renoir (1841–1919), Frédéric Bazille (1841–1870) and Berthe Morisot (1841–1895).
- 1842–1848 First edition of Balzac's *Comédie Humaine*.

1844 Young Paul enters an elementary school in the Rue des Epinaux, Aix, where he remains for five years.

- 1844 At the Paris Salon, Gustave Courbet (1819–1877) exhibits *Lovers in the Country*, *Self-Portrait with a Black Dog* and *The Hammock*; Charles-François Daubigny (1817–1878) exhibits his first landscape of Fontainebleau Forest.
  Alexandre Dumas publishes *The Three Musketeers*.
- 1847–1853 Publication of Michelet's *Histoire de la Révolution française*.

1848 Taking over the Barges Bank in Aix, which had failed, Cézanne's father, with a partner, founds the Cézanne and Cabassol Bank, which prospers.

- 1848 Birth of Paul Gauguin (1848–1903).
  About this time Honoré Daumier (1808–1879) paints *The Riot*, *The Emigrants* and *The Fugitives*.
  Marx and Engels publish the *Communist Manifesto*.
  Monarchy of Louis-Philippe overthrown in February and the Second Republic established. Louis-Napoleon Bonaparte elected President of the Republic in December.

1849 He becomes a day-boarder at the school of Saint-Joseph in Aix, run by a priest, the Abbé Savournin.

- 1849 Courbet paints *A Burial at Ornans*.
  Camille Corot (1796–1875) elected a member of the Salon jury.
  Gustave Flaubert publishes *La Tentation de saint Antoine*.
- 1850 At the Salon, Millet exhibits *The Sower* and Courbet *A Burial at Ornans*: these two painters exemplify the new trend towards realism.
- 1851 Second Republic overthrown by Louis-Napoleon Bonaparte in the *coup d'Etat* of 2 December.

1852 Cézanne enters the Collège Bourbon (now Lycée Mignet) in Aix, where he forms a close friendship with two schoolmates, Baptistin Baille and Emile Zola. Baille, of whom Zola drew a portrait in "L'Oeuvre" (1886), became a professor at the Ecole Polytechnique in Paris; Baille and Cézanne remained friends until 1870.

- 1852 Daubigny paints his *View of the Banks of the Seine*. A friend of Corot and the Barbizon painters, Daubigny also became a friend and supporter of the young Impressionists.
  Louis-Napoleon Bonaparte, becoming the Emperor Napoleon III, founds the Second Empire in France.
- 1853 Birth of Vincent van Gogh (1853–1890).

- 1855 Courbet finishes *The Painter's Studio, A Real Allegory Determining a Phase of Seven Years in my Artistic Life*.
  Paris World's Fair: the jury of the official exhibition refusing Courbet's *A Burial at Ornans* and *The Painter's Studio*, he exhibits them in his own "Pavilion of Realism" erected at his expense.

1856 At the art school in Aix, Cézanne attends the classes of Joseph Gibert. He never forgot the encouragement he received from this teacher as a student and accepted in good part Gibert's later comment on his work: "I can form an idea of the dangers incurred by Painting when I see the outrages you commit." Enthusiasm for music, for Wagner in particular. Long rambles in the Aix countryside with Zola and Baille.

- 1856 Edmond Duranty edits the review *Le Réalisme*.
- 1857 Publication of Flaubert's *Madame Bovary* and Baudelaire's *Les Fleurs du Mal*: both authors are prosecuted for offending against public morals.

1858 Finishes his schooling in Aix and also wins a second prize for drawing at the Ecole des Beaux-Arts. Longs to go to Paris and study painting, but his father enrols him at the law school in Aix. Beginning of his correspondence with Zola, who now goes up to Paris. The family bank prospers and in 1859 his father buys a fine country house just outside Aix, the Jas de Bouffan ("Home of the Winds"), where Cézanne spends his summers and fits up a studio on the top floor.

- 1859 Birth of Georges Seurat (1859–1891).
  Millet finishes *The Angelus*. (Sold for 1,000 francs, it fetched 38,000 francs in 1872 and 553,000 in 1889.)

1860 With the support of his mother and his sister Marie, he tries to obtain his father's permission to study art. Friendship with some local men of note: the sculptor Philippe Solari; the publicist Numa Coste; the painter Achille Emperaire (1829–1898), a man dwarfed by physical deformity, whose painting is akin to that of Monticelli; the journalist Marius Roux; and the critic Antony Valabrègue whose portrait he painted several times. He is influenced by the Caravaggesque pictures in the Aix museum and by the paintings of Emile Loubon (1809–1863), director of the School of Fine Arts in Marseilles.

- 1860 Courbet exhibits successfully at the Salon.
  The first Paris performance of Wagner's *Tannhäuser* is a complete failure.

1861 Despite his father's severe disapproval, he finally obtains the latter's permission to study art in Paris. There, in April, he takes a room in the Rue des Feuillantines on the left bank and works daily at the Académie Suisse, an art school where a nude model is provided but no tuition or guidance. Here he meets Armand Guillaumin (1841–1927) and Camille Pissarro (1830–1903); the latter was to have a beneficial and shaping influence on him in the 1870s. He visits the museums, often with Zola.
In September, after failing the entrance examination at the Ecole des Beaux-Arts, he returns to Aix in a fit of discouragement. He takes a job in his father's bank, but attends drawing classes in the evening. He decorates a room at the Jas de Bouffan with a series of wall paintings, "The Four Seasons."

1861 Ingres, at the age of eighty-one, paints *The Turkish Bath*.
Edouard Manet (1832–1883) makes his first appearance at the Salon.
Birth of Aristide Maillol (1861–1944).

1862 Disliking the work he leaves his father's bank and returns to Paris in November, where once again he works at the Académie Suisse. He makes friends with the Puerto Rican painter Francisco Oller, with whom he broke off relations in 1895, for reasons that are not clear; also with the landscapist Antoine Guillemet (1843–1918) who, while following an official career, never forgot his old friends and it was through his influence that Cézanne was able to exhibit at the Salon in 1882, for the only time in his life. Now too he meets Bazille, Monet, Sisley and Renoir.

1862 Edgar Degas (1834–1917) paints his first pictures of horses and jockeys.
Victor Hugo publishes *Les Misérables* and Flaubert *Salammbô*.

**1863 A picture of his is exhibited at the Salon des Refusés, which he visits with Zola, taking an interest in the controversy aroused by Manet's "Déjeuner sur l'Herbe." The "Salon of the Rejected" was held at the instance of the Emperor himself, so that the public could see the pictures which had been rejected at this year's official Salon by a particularly reactionary jury.
Cézanne begins a series of vehemently romantic compositions. He is much attracted by the work of Courbet and above all by that of Delacroix, who dies in August.**

1863 Birth of Edvard Munch (1863–1944).
Eugène Fromentin publishes his novel *Dominique*.

1864 In a momentary fit of discouragement he again returns to Aix. From now on he divides his time between Aix and Paris.

1864 Birth of Henri de Toulouse-Lautrec (1864–1901).
Corot becomes a member of the admission committee at the Salon.

1865 Cézanne submits a canvas to the Salon: it is refused. The first public mention of Cézanne as a painter occurs in a review by Marius Roux of Zola's novel "La Confession de Claude."

1866 Again his work is rejected at the Salon. To the Superintendent of Fine Arts, Count Emilien de Nieuwerkerke (1811–1892), he writes two letters of protest calling for the re-establishment of the Salon des Refusés: both go unanswered. Nieuwerkerke, not only an administrator but a highly successful sculptor, carves flattering busts and statues of the Emperor and Empress and moves in the highest circles of Parisian society.

1866 Courbet's work acclaimed at the Salon.
The Café Guerbois, in the Batignolles quarter of Paris, becomes the meeting place of the younger artists and writers, prominent among them being Manet and the future Impressionists; Cézanne makes only a very occasional appearance. Here the idea of a group exhibition of independent artists was first broached and discussed. Several books evoke the atmosphere and talk of the evenings spent in this café in the 1860s: Armand Silvestre's *Au Pays des Souvenirs*, Emile Zola's *L'Oeuvre* and Edmond Duranty's *La Double Vie de Louis Segond*.

1867– Up to the time of the Franco-Prussian War, he is continually moving to and fro between Provence and Paris, 1870 seldom staying long at the same address. He paints exuberant, baroque compositions on erotic themes: "The Rape," "The Orgy," "The Temptation of St Anthony." He begins living with a young woman, Hortense Fiquet, but takes care to conceal this liaison from his father; they were not married until 1886. To avoid conscription in 1870, Cézanne withdraws to L'Estaque, a village on the Mediterranean coast about fifteen miles from Aix.

1867 Death of Baudelaire, Ingres and Théodore Rousseau (1812–1867).
Birth of Pierre Bonnard (1867–1947).
Paris World's Fair. Courbet and Manet, avoiding the official exhibition, show their work in private pavilions erected at their own expense in the Rond-Point de l'Alma.
Monet paints *Women in the Garden*. Corot is made an Officer of the Legion of Honour.
The Goncourt brothers publish *Manette Salomon*, a novel about the painters of the Barbizon school.

1868 Manet paints his *Portrait of Zola* and Renoir his *Portrait of Alfred Sisley and His Wife*.

1869 Renoir and Monet work at Bougival, a village on the Seine downstream from Paris, one of the birthplaces of Impressionism: their famous pictures of La Grenouillère ("The Frog-Pond"), a popular bathing spot at Bougival, were painted the same day, at the same time.
Birth of Henri Matisse (1869–1954).
Death of Alphonse de Lamartine.

1870 18 July: France declares war on Prussia.
During the war Cézanne works at L'Estaque; Daubigny, Monet and Pissarro take refuge in London; Bazille is killed in battle at Beaune-la-Rolande on 28 November.
1 September: Decisive defeat of the French armies at Sedan, the Emperor being taken prisoner. Proclamation of the Third Republic on 4 September.

1871 Soon after the armistice (28 January) Cézanne returns to Paris.

1871 The Paris Commune (1 March–28 May).
Birth of Georges Rouault (1871–1958).
Rimbaud writes *Le Bateau ivre*.
Zola publishes *La Fortune des Rougon*, the first volume of the Rougon-Macquart series, his great cycle of twenty novels depicting French life and society during the Second Empire.
Adolphe Thiers elected President of the Republic by the National Assembly.

1872 Birth in Paris of Cézanne's son Paul (4 January). In the spring, with Hortense and the child, he joins Pissarro at Pontoise, twenty miles northwest of Paris, where he stays at the Auberge du Grand Cerf. In the autumn he moves to Auvers-sur-Oise, a few miles away, where he stays with Dr Paul Gachet, an art-loving homoeopath and former habitué of the Café Guerbois, himself an amateur painter and etcher; he was one of the first collectors of Cézanne's work. Cézanne remains at Auvers until the spring of 1874.

1872 Monet paints *Impression, Sunrise*, the picture that two years later gave its name to Impressionism.

1873 At Auvers he paints "The Hanged Man's House" and many landscapes. There and at Pontoise, working alongside Pissarro, he is initiated into the impressionist technique. In Paris he makes the acquaintance of Julien Tanguy,

better known as Père Tanguy, who as an itinerant colour-grinder in the 1860s had already met most of the younger painters. As an idealistic socialist, Tanguy had joined the Commune in 1871; after it was crushed, he was arrested and deported. Now, on his return to Paris, he opened his famous colour-shop in the Rue Clauzel, where he supplied the Impressionists. Generous and disinterested, he often gave his colours in exchange for pictures, and for many years his shop was the only place where Cézanne paintings could be seen and purchased.

1873　On his return from a voyage to New Orleans (where his brother René is a cotton broker), Degas paints dancers and themes of modern life, treated in bright colours. Monet paints river scenes at Argenteuil and fits up a studio-boat on the Seine. Renoir settles in Montmartre. Manet paints at Berck-sur-Mer on the Channel coast.

　　　　Rimbaud writes *Une Saison en Enfer*.

　　　　Thiers is forced to resign and MacMahon is elected President of the Republic.

　　　　Napoleon III dies in exile at Chislehurst, near London.

1874　At the insistence of Pissarro, despite the opposition of many other exhibitors, Cézanne takes part in the first group exhibition of the Impressionists, held in the studios of the photographer Nadar, at 35 Boulevard des Capucines. His two canvases, "The Hanged Man's House" (purchased at the exhibition for 300 francs by Count Armand Doria) and "A Modern Olympia," are the ones that arouse most derision and hostility.

1875　Living in Paris on the Quai d'Anjou, Ile Saint-Louis. Through Renoir he meets Victor Chocquet, an official in the customs administration and an enlightened collector of paintings. Their common admiration for Delacroix seals their friendship at once. On friendly terms with all the Impressionists, especially with Renoir, Chocquet from now on does much to defend their work and make it better known to public and critics.

1875　Impressionist auction sale at the Hôtel Drouot, Paris.

　　　　Death of Millet and Corot.

1876　Spends the summer painting at L'Estaque. Refuses to take part in the second group exhibition of the Impressionists.

1877　Works at Pontoise and Auvers-sur-Oise. He shows seventeen canvases (still lifes and landscapes) at the third group exhibition, but the public is as hostile as ever to his work. Cézanne took no further part in the subsequent exhibitions of the impressionist group.

1877　During the third impressionist exhibition, in April, their friend George Rivière publishes a weekly paper, *L'Impressionniste*, describing and commenting on the show.

　　　　Death of Courbet.

1878　He spends the year in the South of France, first in Marseilles, where he installs Hortense Fiquet and his son, then at Aix and L'Estaque. His father, discovering the existence of Hortense and little Paul, is furious and reduces his allowance, so that Cézanne is hard put to make ends meet.

1878　Paris World's Fair. Théodore Duret publishes *Les Peintres impressionnistes*, "the first authoritative attempt to explain impressionism and to single out its leaders" (John Rewald).

1879　After a stay of several months at Melun with Hortense and Paul, he goes to Paris, then spends June with Zola at the latter's newly acquired house at Médan, on the Seine. The pictures he submits to the Salon are regularly refused.

1879　Death of Daumier.

　　　　Birth of Paul Klee (1879–1940).

1880　Several months in Paris; then, during the summer, he again stays with Zola at Médan.

1880　Zola publishes *Nana*.

　　　　Publication of *Les Soirées de Médan*, a set of six tales by six naturalist writers (Zola, Maupassant, Huysmans, Henry Céard, Léon Hennique, Paul Alexis), all dealing with the events of 1870.

　　　　Death of Flaubert.

1881　From May to November he again works at Pontoise with Pissarro and there meets Gauguin. After a short visit to Zola at Médan, he returns to Aix in November.
In the spring his younger sister Rose marries Maxime Conil, a native of Aix. (His elder sister Marie remained unmarried.)

1881　Birth of Pablo Picasso (1881–1973).

1882　Thanks to his friend Guillemet, who is a member of the jury, a portrait of his is accepted at the Salon. Renoir, on his way home from a trip to Italy, pays him a visit at L'Estaque in February. After some months in Paris, Cézanne returns for a time to his father's house, Le Jas de Bouffan, near Aix.

1882　Courbet retrospective exhibition at the Ecole des Beaux-Arts, Paris.

　　　　Birth of Georges Braque (1882–1963).

1883　Works around Aix and at L'Estaque, from May to November, often with Adolphe Monticelli (1824–1886). Renoir and Monet pay him a visit in December.

1883　Paul Durand-Ruel, the first dealer to take up the Impressionists, holds a series of one-man shows in his Paris gallery: Monet, Renoir, Pissarro, and Sisley. Durand-Ruel also organizes an impressionist exhibition in London at Dowdeswell's galleries in New Bond Street.

　　　　Seurat's first appearance at the Salon.

　　　　Death of Manet.

　　　　Birth of Maurice Utrillo (1883–1955).

1884　Founding of the Society of Independent Artists and the Salon des Indépendants, where Seurat exhibits *Bathing at Asnières*.

　　　　Pissarro settles at Eragny, near Gisors (Eure).

　　　　Manet retrospective at the Ecole des Beaux-Arts, Paris.

　　　　J. K. Huysmans publishes *A Rebours* and Paul Verlaine *Jadis* and *Naguère*.

1885　Stays with Renoir at La Roche-Guyon, apparently recovering from the emotional shock of a mysterious, abortive love-affair with a woman of Aix. Then, after working at Villennes (near Pontoise) and Vernon (near Giverny), he stays with Chocquet at the latter's summer home at Hattenville, Normandy. During the summer he also pays a visit to Zola at Médan.

1885　Pissarro meets Paul Signac (1863–1935) and Seurat and adopts Pointillism the following year. Renoir works on his *Large Bathers* (Philadelphia).

　　　　Van Gogh works at Nuenen (Dutch Brabant).

　　　　Zola publishes *Germinal* and Maupassant *Bel-Ami*.

1886　In March appears Zola's new novel "L'Oeuvre" ("His Masterpiece"), whose hero, Claude Lantier, is an unsuccessful painter obviously modelled on Cézanne. The

long friendship that had bound painter and writer together since their school days in Aix is now broken off, never to be resumed.

At Aix, on 20 April, he marries Hortense Fiquet, with his father's consent; the latter dies a few months later at the age of eighty-eight. When the estate was settled, Cézanne's share amounted to 400,000 francs, making him now independent.

1886   Eighth and last group exhibition of the Impressionists in Paris. Durand-Ruel organizes an impressionist exhibition in New York at the National Academy of Design. Van Gogh arrives in Paris. Gauguin makes his first stay at Pont-Aven in Brittany.

Revelation of the Douanier Rousseau (1844–1910) at the Salon des Indépendants.

The critic Félix Fénéon publishes *Les Impressionnistes en 1886* and Rimbaud *Les Illuminations*.

1887   **He spends most of the year at Aix, painting in the open air in the surrounding countryside, chiefly in the neighbourhood of an old farmstead known as the Château Noir, on the Route du Tholonet, where he rents a room to store his painting gear. He works much around the near-by Bibémus quarry, where he also rents a small house which he uses as a studio.**

1887   Lautrec and Van Gogh momentarily adopt the pointillist technique.

Birth of Juan Gris (1887–1927) and Marc Chagall.

Sadi Carnot elected President of the Republic.

1888   **Cézanne makes a five-month stay at the Hôtel de la Cour at Chantilly, some twenty miles north of Paris, where he paints the fine alleys of trees leading to the Château. Several painting excursions in the Ile-de-France.**

1888   After two years in Paris, Van Gogh moves to Arles. Gauguin works at Pont-Aven with Emile Bernard (1868–1941), where they develop the new style of heavily contoured forms and flat colours which they call Synthetism or Cloisonnism.

The young artists soon to be known as the Nabis (Sérusier, Bonnard, Vuillard) meet at the Académie Julian, Paris.

In London George Moore publishes his *Confessions of a Young Man*, which gives some glimpses of the Impressionists, in particular Manet and Degas, whom Moore knew well.

1889   **Renoir, with his wife and his son Pierre, pays a visit to Cézanne in Aix, staying with him at the home of Cézanne's brother-in-law Maxime Conil at Montbriant, an estate not far from the Jas de Bouffan.**

His friend Chocquet, who had bought the picture from Count Doria, contrives to have his "Hanged Man's House" included in the exhibition of French painting held in connection with the Paris World's Fair.

1889   Exhibition of pictures by Gauguin and his friends at the Café Volpini during the Paris World's Fair. Construction of the Eiffel Tower.

1890   **Invited to exhibit in Brussels with the group known as Les XX (The Twenty), Cézanne sends in three pictures: a study of bathers, "Thatched House at Auvers" and a landscape.**

First symptoms of diabetes, which was to trouble him in later years.

1890   Pissarro abandons Pointillism, and Renoir abandons his linear, Ingresque style.

Monet's first series of pictures on a single motif, "Poplars" and "Haystacks" to begin with.

Van Gogh commits suicide at Auvers-sur-Oise.

The literary review *Mercure de France* launched by Alfred Vallette.

1891   **With his wife and son, Cézanne makes a two-month trip through the French Jura and on to Switzerland, staying at Neuchâtel, Geneva, Lausanne, Vevey, Berne and Fribourg —his only trip abroad.**

1891   Gauguin sails for Tahiti.

First group show of the Nabis (Galerie Le Barc de Boutteville, Paris).

Van Gogh retrospective at the Salon des Indépendants.

Puvis de Chavannes commissioned to paint murals for the Boston Public Library.

Founding of the *Revue Blanche* by the Natanson brothers, intimate friends of Lautrec and the Nabis.

Death of Seurat at the age of thirty-two.

1892   **Cézanne divides his time between Aix and Paris, also making a stay at Fontainebleau. A very productive year, at work on different versions of "Card Players," "Bathers" and "Mont Sainte-Victoire."**

1892   Seurat retrospective sponsored by the *Revue Blanche*.

Renoir and Pissarro exhibitions at the Durand-Ruel gallery.

Matisse becomes a pupil of Gustave Moreau at the Ecole des Beaux-Arts, Paris.

1893   Ambroise Vollard opens his gallery in the Rue Laffitte, Paris.

Rouault and Matisse become acquainted, as fellow students in Gustave Moreau's studio.

Zola completes the Rougon-Macquart cycle of novels.

Birth of Joan Miró.

Publication in London and New York of George Moore's *Modern Painting*, dealing at length with the Impressionists.

1894   **On a visit to Monet at the latter's home at Giverny, Cézanne meets Clemenceau, Rodin and the critic Gustave Geffroy. Of the latter, he paints one of his finest portraits in 1895. Geffroy this year publishes his "History of Impressionism"; this book and his articles do much to break down the rooted prejudice against Cézanne and the Impressionists.**

1894   Death of Gustave Caillebotte (1848–1894), a close friend of the group, who bequeathes his fine collection of impressionist paintings to the French State: it includes two Cézannes, three Manets, sixteen Monets, eight Renoirs, thirteen Pissarros, seven Degas's and eight Sisleys. The Caillebotte bequest arouses a public controversy, the hidebound officials then in charge of the French museums doing their best to refuse it. In the end, only part of the collection is accepted: it forms the nucleus of the impressionist collection now in the Jeu de Paume museum, Place de la Concorde, Paris.

In the United States, publication of Hamlin Garland's *Crumbling Idols*, containing a defence of the Impressionists, one of the first to be written in English, likening them to "skilled musicians; the actual working out of the melody is rapid, but it has taken vast study and practice."

In France, Captain Alfred Dreyfus is convicted of espionage on false evidence and deported to Devil's Island.

Sadi Carnot, President of the Republic, assassinated by an anarchist in Lyons on 24 June. Elected to replace him, Jean Casimir-Périer is forced to resign in January 1895.

1895 Cézanne's first one-man exhibition organized by Ambroise Vollard in his Rue Laffitte gallery. Geffroy reviews it in glowing terms. Pissarro writes to his son Lucien: "My enthusiasm is nothing compared with Renoir's. Even Degas has succumbed to the charm of this refined savage. Monet, all of us..." But the public continues to find his work incomprehensible.

1896 Beginning of Cézanne's friendship with a young poet of Aix, Joachim Gasquet, the son of a boyhood friend of his, Henri Gasquet, a local baker. In June he does a cure at Vichy, then spends part of the summer at Talloires on the Lake of Annecy, in Savoy.

1896 Pissarro paints views of Rouen, on the lower Seine.
Death of Verlaine and Edmond de Goncourt.

1897 He spends part of the spring painting in Fontainebleau Forest.
Death of his mother, aged eighty-two, at the Jas de Bouffan in October.

1897 Exhibitions of impressionist paintings in London and Stockholm.
Zola's first article in defence of Captain Dreyfus published in *Le Figaro*.

1898 Most of the year in Aix. In the autumn he goes up to Paris and then works for a while at Montgeroult, near Pontoise. Second Cézanne exhibition at Vollard's.

1898 Death of Mallarmé, Gustave Moreau (1826–1898), Puvis de Chavannes (1824–1898) and Eugène Boudin (1824–1898).
Death of Victor Chocquet, whose collection includes by now thirty-two Cézannes.
In the Paris daily *L'Aurore* of 13 January, Zola publishes an open letter to the President of the Republic, beginning with the words *J'accuse*, a terrible denunciation of all those who had had a hand in the conspiracy against the innocent Dreyfus.

1899 For reasons that are not clear, Cézanne sells the Jas de Bouffan estate and moves into a small flat in the centre of Aix (23 Rue Boulegon), where he remains until his death, looked after by a faithful housekeeper, Madame Brémond. His wife and his son Paul live chiefly in Paris.
Three of his paintings are exhibited in Paris at the Salon des Indépendants.

1899 Nabi exhibition at the Durand-Ruel gallery.
Paul Signac publishes *D'Eugène Delacroix au néo-impressionnisme*, an important study of the modern movement.
Death of Alfred Sisley (1839–1899).

1900 At the Paris Centennial Exposition of French Art, Cézanne is represented by three canvases. His fame is growing and he is beginning to be known even outside France.

1900 Triumph of Art Nouveau at the Paris World's Fair.
Seurat retrospective on the premises of the *Revue Blanche*.
Picasso's first visit to Paris, where Braque, Léger and Dufy are art students.

1901 He exhibits two pictures at the Salon des Indépendants, Paris, and two more at the Salon de la Libre Esthétique, Brussels.
At the end of the year he buys a piece of ground on the Chemin des Lauves, a few miles north of Aix, where he has a studio built.

1901 Maurice Denis (1870–1943) exhibits at the Salon his famous picture *Homage to Cézanne*.
Van Gogh retrospective at the Bernheim-Jeune gallery.
Death of Toulouse-Lautrec.

1902 Friendship with a young writer, Léo Larguier; he spends the autumn in the Cévennes with Larguier.
Despite the breach of their friendship, Cézanne is much affected by the death of Zola (29 September), accidentally asphyxiated in his Paris flat.
The writer Octave Mirbeau, whom Cézanne admired, intervenes on his behalf and tries to obtain the Legion of Honour decoration for him: the officials concerned refuse to grant it.

1902 Toulouse-Lautrec retrospective at the Salon des Indépendants.
Picasso exhibitions in the Paris galleries of Vollard and Berthe Weill; the latter also holds a Matisse exhibition.

1903 Frantz Jourdain founds the Salon d'Automne, which opens with a Gauguin retrospective, following Gauguin's death (8 May) at Atuana in the Marquesas Islands.
Gertrude Stein and her brothers Leo and Michael settle in Paris and soon begin buying Cézannes and Renoirs; from 1905, they buy paintings by Matisse and Picasso.
Impressionist and Neo-Impressionist exhibition at the Vienna Secession.
Death of Pissarro.

1904 Pays his last visit to Paris and paints for the last time at Fontainebleau. An entire room is set aside for his work at the Salon d'Automne, thirty-three pictures being exhibited: general recognition and acclaim come to him for the first time. He exhibits nine canvases in Brussels at the Salon de la Libre Esthétique. He becomes friendly with the painter Emile Bernard, who had seen Cézanne's canvases years before in Père Tanguy's colour-shop and now seeks him out in Aix.

1904 Renoir retrospective at the Salon d'Automne.
Matisse's first one-man show held at the Vollard gallery.
Picasso settles in Paris for good.

1905 Cézanne again exhibits at the Salon d'Automne and at the Salon des Indépendants. He completes the "Large Bathers" on which he had been working for years.

1905 Manet retrospective and Fauve room at the Salon d'Automne; Seurat and Van Gogh retrospectives at the Salon des Indépendants.
Major impressionist exhibition in London at the Grafton Galleries.

1906 Cézanne shows ten canvases at the Salon d'Automne. On 15 October, while working in the Aix countryside on his picture "Le Cabanon de Jourdan," he is caught in a heavy rainstorm. Drenched and chilled, he collapses by the roadside as he tries to seek shelter; there he is found by the driver of a passing laundry-cart, who brings him home to the Rue Boulegon. By an effort of will he rises again the next day and works on his last portrait of Vallier, his gardener. But pneumonia has set in and he dies on 22 October, at the age of sixty-seven.

1906 Gauguin retrospective at the Salon d'Automne.
Picasso begins work on the *Demoiselles d'Avignon*.

1907 A memorial exhibition of fifty-six of his paintings is held in Paris at the Salon d'Automne.

Bibliography

Catalogues

L. VENTURI, *Cézanne, son art, son œuvre*, 2 vols., Paris 1936. – A. CHAPPUIS, *The Drawings of Paul Cézanne, A Catalogue Raisonné*, 2 vols., Greenwich, Conn. 1973. – A new catalogue of the paintings and watercolours is being prepared by John REWALD.

Correspondence and Witness Accounts

M. ROUX, "La Confession de Claude par Emile Zola," *Memorial d'Aix*, December 1865. – E. ZOLA, *Mon Salon*, Paris 1866, 1970; "Le naturalisme au Salon," *Le Voltaire*, June 1880; *L'Oeuvre*, Paris 1886; *Correspondance, Lettres de jeunesse*, Paris 1907. – J.K. HUYSMANS, "Trois peintres: Cézanne, Tissot, Wagner," in *Certains*, Paris 1889. – E. BERNARD, "Paul Cézanne," *Les Hommes d'aujourd'hui*, 1892; "Paul Cézanne," *L'Occident*, July 1904; "Souvenirs sur Paul Cézanne et lettres inédites," *Mercure de France*, October 1907. – G. GEFFROY, "Paul Cézanne," *Le Journal*, March 1894. – T. NATANSON, "Paul Cézanne," *Revue Blanche*, December 1895. – A. FONTAINAS, "Exposition Cézanne," *Mercure de France*, June 1898. – F. FAGUS, "Quarante tableaux de Cézanne," *Revue Blanche*, December 1899. – G. LECOMTE, "Paul Cézanne," *Revue d'Art*, December 1899. – "Paul Cézanne. Quatre lettres sur la peinture à Charles Camoin présentées par G.A." (Apollinaire), *Les Soirées de Paris*, 1904. – M. DENIS, "Cézanne," *L'Ermitage*, November 1905. – C. MORICE, "Aquarelles de Cézanne," *Mercure de France*, July 1905; "Mort de Paul Cézanne," *Mercure de France*, November 1906. – L. VAUXCELLES, "Cézanne," *Gil Blas*, March 1905. – J. ROYÈRE, "Sur Paul Cézanne," *La Phalange*, November 1906. – A. VOLLARD, *Paul Cézanne*, Paris 1914, New York 1923. – E. JALOUX, "Souvenirs sur Paul Cézanne," *L'Amour de l'Art*, 1920. – K. OSTHAUS, "Cézanne," *Das Feuer*, 1920 and *Marianne*, February 1939. – E. BERNARD, *Souvenirs sur Paul Cézanne*, Paris 1921. – C. CAMOIN, "Souvenirs sur Paul Cézanne," *L'Amour de l'Art*, January 1921. – J. GASQUET, *Cézanne*, Paris 1921. – M. LAFARGUE, "Souvenirs sur Cézanne," *L'Amour de l'Art*, January 1921. – L. LARGUIER, *Le dimanche avec Paul Cézanne*, Paris 1925. – *Correspondance*, edited by J. REWALD, Paris 1937, 1960; *Letters*, London-New York 1941. – L. VENTURI, *Les Archives de l'Impressionnisme*, 2 vols., Paris-New York 1939. – R.M. RILKE, *Briefe aus den Jahren 1906–1907*; *Lettres sur Cézanne*, Paris 1944. – C. PISSARRO, *Letters to His Son Lucien*, New York 1943; *Lettres à son fils Lucien*, Paris 1950.

Monographs and Critical Studies

T. DURET, *Les peintres impressionnistes*, Paris 1878; new ed., *Histoire des peintres impressionnistes*, Paris 1906. – G. GEFFROY, *Histoire de l'impressionnisme*, Paris 1894. – R. MARX, *Un siècle d'art*, Paris 1900. – E. FAURE, *Paul Cézanne*, Paris 1910, 1936. – J. MEIER-GRAEFE, *Cézanne und seine Ahnen*, Munich 1910. – J. RIVIÈRE, *Etudes*, Paris 1910. – M. DENIS, *Théories*, Paris 1912. – F. BURGER, *Cézanne und Hodler*, Munich 1913. – *Cézanne*, Paris 1914 (essays by O. Mirbeau, T. Duret, L. Werth, F. Jourdain, G. Bernheim-Jeune). – G. COQUIOT, *Paul Cézanne*, Paris 1919. – W. BARTH, *Paul Cézanne*, Basel 1921. – J. MEIER-GRAEFE, *Cézanne und sein Kreis*, Munich 1922. – H. von WEDDERKOP, *Paul Cézanne*, Leipzig 1922. – T. KLINGSOR, *Cézanne*, Paris 1923. – P. MURATOV, *Cézanne*, Berlin 1923. – G. RIVIÈRE, *Le maître Paul Cézanne*, Paris 1923. – A. SALMON, *Cézanne*, Paris 1923. – W. GEORGE, *Les aquarelles de Cézanne*, Paris 1926. – L. VENTURI, *Il gusto dei primitivi*, Bologna 1926. – R. FRY, *Cézanne, A Study of His Development*, London-New York 1927. – K. PFISTER, *Paul Cézanne*, Potsdam 1927. – E. d'ORS, *Cézanne*, Paris 1930, London 1936. – H. GRANVILLE FELL, *Cézanne, A Pioneer of Modern Painting*, London-Edinburgh 1933. – S. LÉVY, *Cézanne*, Paris 1933. – G. RIVIÈRE, *Cézanne, le peintre solitaire*, Paris 1933. – N. JAVORSKAIA, *Paul Cézanne*, Milan 1935. – G. MACK, *Paul Cézanne*, New York-London 1935. – R. HUYGHE, *Cézanne*, Paris 1936. – L. LARGUIER, *Paul Cézanne ou le drame de la peinture*, Paris 1936. – M. RAYNAL, *Initiation à l'art moderne. Cézanne*, Paris 1936. – F. NOVOTNY, *Cézanne*, Vienna 1937. – A. CHAPPUIS, *Dessins de Paul Cézanne*, Paris 1938. – F. NOVOTNY, *Cézanne und das Ende der wissenschaftlichen Perspektive*, Vienna 1938. – A. VOLLARD, *En écoutant Cézanne, Degas, Renoir*, Paris 1938. – J. REWALD, *Cézanne, sa vie, son œuvre, son amitié pour Zola*, Paris 1939; *Paul Cézanne*, New York 1948. – A.C. BARNES and V. de MAZIA, *The Art of Cézanne*, New York 1939. – R. COGNIAT, *Cézanne*, Paris 1939. – G. JEDLICKA, *Cézanne*, Zürich-Leipzig 1939. – E. LORAN, *Cézanne's Composition, Analysis of His Form with Diagrams and Photographs of His Motifs*, Berkeley-Los Angeles 1943. – L. VENTURI, *Cézanne, Water Colours*, London 1943. – E.A. JEWELL, *Cézanne*, New York 1944. – J. REWALD, *The History of Impressionism*, New York 1946; 4th ed., 1973. – G. SCHILDT, *Le comportement psychologique de Cézanne, interprétation de son art et de sa personnalité*, Stockholm 1946. – B. DORIVAL, *Cézanne*, Paris-New York 1948. – A. LHOTE, *Cézanne*, Lausanne 1949. – L. GUERRY, *Cézanne et l'expression de l'espace*, Paris 1950. – F. JOURDAIN, *Cézanne*, Paris 1950. – F. NOVOTNY, "Cézanne als Zeichner," *Wiener Jahrbuch für Kunstgeschichte*, Vienna 1950. – L. VENTURI, *Da Manet a Lautrec*, Florence 1950, Paris 1953. – J. REWALD, *Paul Cézanne, Carnets de Dessins*, Paris 1951. – P. GACHET, *Cézanne à Auvers, Cézanne graveur*, Paris 1952. – M. SCHAPIRO, *Cézanne*, New York 1952; new ed., 1965. – H.L. SHERMAN, *Cézanne and Visual Form*, Columbus, Ohio 1952. – G. SCHMIDT, *Aquarelles de Paul Cézanne*, Basel 1952. – M. RAYNAL, *Cézanne*, Geneva-New York 1954. – K. BADT, *Die Kunst Cézannes*, Munich 1956; *The Art of Cézanne*, Berkeley-Los Angeles 1965. – H. PERRUCHOT, *La vie de Cézanne*, Paris 1956. – L. VENTURI, *Four Steps Toward Modern Art*, New York 1956. – A. CHAPPUIS, *Dessins de Cézanne*, Lausanne 1957. – G. BERTHOLD, *Cézanne und die alten Meister*, Stuttgart 1958. – A. NEUMEYER, *Cézanne Drawings*, New York-London 1958. – J. LETHÈVE, *Impressionnistes et Symbolistes devant la presse*, Paris 1959. – L. HANSON, *Mortal Victory, A Biography of Paul Cézanne*, New York-London 1960. – A. CHAPPUIS, *Les dessins de Paul Cézanne*, Lausanne 1962. – S. LONGSTREET, *Paul Cézanne, Drawings*, Los Angeles 1964. – A. CHAPPUIS, *Album de Paul Cézanne*, Paris 1966. – A. MARTINI and R. NEGRI, *Cézanne e il post-impressionismo*, Milan 1967. – F. ELGAR, *Cézanne*, Paris 1968. – M. de MICHELI, *Cézanne*, Florence 1968. – R.W. MURPHY, *The World of Cézanne*, New York 1968. – R.J. NIESS, *Zola, Cézanne and Manet. A Study of L'Oeuvre*, Ann Arbor, Michigan 1968. – N. PONENTE, *Paul Cézanne*, Milan 1968. – F.H. LEM, *Paul Cézanne. Etude thématique et critique de l'œuvre*, Paris 1969. – J. LINDSAY, *Cézanne, His Life and Art*, London and Greenwich, Conn. 1969. – W.V. ANDERSEN, *Cézanne's Portrait Drawings*, Cambridge, Mass. and London 1970. – M. HOOG, *L'Univers de Cézanne*, Paris 1971. – J. LEYMARIE and M. MELOT, *Les Gravures des Impressionnistes*, Paris 1971. – J. SIBLIK, *Paul Cézanne, Dessins*, Paris 1972. – J. CHERPIN, *Paul Cézanne, l'œuvre gravé*, Marseilles 1972. – S. COTTE, *Cézanne*, Paris 1974. – M. BRION, *Paul Cézanne*, New York-London 1975. – S. ORIENTI, *The Complete Paintings of Cézanne*, New York-London 1975.

Articles and Reviews

L. LEROY, "L'exposition des impressionnistes," *Charivari*, April 1874. – P. MANTZ, "L'exposition des peintres impressionnistes," *Le Temps*, April 1877. – G. RIVIÈRE, "L'exposition des impressionnistes," *L'Impressionniste, Journal d'Art*, April 1877. – J.E. BLANCHE, "Le Salon d'Automne," *Mercure de France*, 1904. – C. MORICE, "Enquête sur les tendances actuelles des arts plastiques," *Mercure de France*, August-September 1905. – M. DENIS, "Cézanne," *L'Occident*, September 1907. – C. MORICE, "Cézanne," *Mercure de France*, February 1907. – R.P. RIVIÈRE and J.F. SCHNERB, "L'atelier de Cézanne," *La Grande Revue*, December 1907. – A. ALEXANDRE, "L'œuvre de Paul Cézanne," *Comoedia*, January 1910. – C. MORICE, "Exposition d'œuvres de Cézanne," *Mercure de France*, February 1910. – E. FAURE, "Paul Cézanne," *L'Art Décoratif*, October 1911. – A. GLEIZES, "La tradition et le cubisme," *Montjoie!*, February 1913. – G. KAHN, "Aquarelles de Cézanne," *Mercure de France*, December 1913. – A. VOLLARD, "Paul Cézanne," *La Vie*, November 1913. – "Sedici opere di Cézanne, Maestri moderni," *La Voce*, 1914. – E. BERNARD, "La méthode de Paul Cézanne," *Mercure de France*, March 1920. – L. HENRAUX, "I Cézanne della raccolta Fabbri," *Dedalo*, 1920. – A. LHOTE, "L'enseignement de Cézanne," *Nouvelle Revue Française*, November 1920. – G. SEVERINI, "Cézanne et le cézannisme," *L'Esprit Nouveau*, November-December 1921. – A. TABARANT, "Cézanne," *Bulletin* de la Vie artistique, August 1921. – F.J. FRIEDLÄNDER, "Über Paul Cézanne," Die Kunst, February 1922. – É. BERNARD, "Les aquarelles de Cézanne," L'Amour de l'Art, February 1924. – M. DENIS, "Le dessin de Cézanne," L'Amour de l'Art, February 1924. – J.G. GOULINAT, "L'évolution du métier de Cézanne," L'Art Vivant, March 1925. – G. RIVIÈRE, "La formation de Paul Cézanne," L'Amour de l'Art, August 1925. – R. FRY, "Le développement de Cézanne," L'Amour de l'Art, December 1926. – A. SALMON, "Dessins inédits de Cézanne," Cahiers d'Art, 1926. – F. NOVOTNY, "Paul Cézanne," Belvedere, 1929. – D. LEBLOND-ZOLA, "Zola et Cézanne, d'après une correspondance retrouvée," Mercure de France, January 1931. – F. NOVOTNY, "Das Problem des Menschen Cézanne im Verhältnis zu seiner Kunst," Zeitschrift für Ästhetik und allgemeine Kunstwissenschaft, 1932. – C. ZERVOS, "Renoir. Cézanne. Leurs contemporains et la jeune peinture anglaise," Cahiers d'Art, 1934. – L. VENTURI, "Paul Cézanne," L'Arte, May-September 1935. – J. REWALD and L. MARSCHUTZ, "Cézanne und der Jas de Bouffan," Forum, 1935. – L. DOUGLAS, "Paul Cézanne," The Burlington Magazine, 1936. – L. GILLET, "Le mystère Cézanne," Revue des Deux Mondes, 1936. – A. LHOTE, "Cézanne l'incompris," Nouvelle Revue Française, 1936. – E. d'ORS, "Crise de Cézanne," Gazette des Beaux-Arts, 1936. – L. VENTURI, "Sur les dernières années de Cézanne," Minotaure, 1936. – G. WILDENSTEIN, "Cézanne," Gazette des Beaux-Arts, 1936. – A.H. BARR, "Cézanne d'après les lettres de Marion à Morstatt," Gazette des Beaux-Arts, January 1937; "Cézanne in the Letters of Marion to Morstatt, 1865–68," Magazine of Art, February-May 1938. – J. REWALD, "A propos du catalogue raisonné de l'œuvre de Cézanne et de la chronologie de cette œuvre," La Renaissance, March-April 1937. – L. VENTURI, "The Early Style of Cézanne," Parnassus, March 1937. – G. BAZIN, "Cézanne et la Montagne Sainte-Victoire," L'Amour de l'Art, June 1938. – J. REWALD, "Achille Emperaire, ami de Paul Cézanne," L'Amour de l'Art, May 1938; "Paul Cézanne: nouveaux documents sur les années 1870–1871," The Burlington Magazine, April 1939. – D. LEBLOND-ZOLA, "Paul Alexis, ami des peintres," Mercure de France, March 1939. – K. BADT, "Cézanne's Watercolour Technique," The Burlington Magazine, October 1943. – J. GORIANY, "Cézanne's lithograph The Small Bathers," Gazette des Beaux-Arts, 1943. – G. BAZIN, "Cézanne devant l'impressionnisme," Labyrinthe, February 1945. – M. MERLEAU-PONTY, "Le doute de Cézanne," Les Temps modernes, 1946. – J. BOUCHOT-SAUPIQUE, "Un carnet de croquis de Cézanne," La Revue des Arts, 1951. – D. COOPER, "Two Cézanne Exhibitions," The Burlington Magazine, 1954; "Au Jas de Bouffan," L'Oeil, February 1955. – H. PERRUCHOT, "Les quinze logis de Monsieur Cézanne," L'Oeil, 1955. – L. GOWING, "Notes on the Development of Cézanne," The Burlington Magazine, 1956. – C. GRAY, "Cézanne's Use of Perspective," The College Art Journal, 1959. – T. REFF, "Cézanne: The Enigma of the Nude," Art News, November 1959. – B. BARILLI, "Gli Impressionisti, Cézanne e alcune teorie della percezione," Palatina, 1960. – C. FLORY-BLONDEL, "Quelques souvenirs sur Paul Cézanne," Gazette des Beaux-Arts, 1960. – T. REFF, "Cézanne and Poussin," Journal of the Warburg and Courtauld Institutes, 1960; "A New Exhibition of Cézanne," The Burlington Magazine, 1960; "Reproductions and Books in Cézanne's Studio," Gazette des Beaux-Arts, 1960. – A. MASSON, "Paul Cézanne et l'olivier," Style, 1961. – M. BODELSEN, "Gauguin's Cézanne," The Burlington Magazine, May 1962. – T. REFF, "Cézanne's Bather with Outstretched Arms," Gazette des Beaux-Arts, 1962; "Cézanne and Flaubert," The Art Bulletin, 1962. – M. WALDFOGEL, "A Problem in Cézanne's Grandes Baigneuses," The Burlington Magazine, 1962. – R. WALTER, "Cézanne à Bonnecourt en 1866," Gazette des Beaux-Arts, 1962; "Un vrai Cézanne: La vue de Bonnières," Gazette des Beaux-Arts, 1963. – S. LICHTENSTEIN, "Cézanne and Delacroix," The Art Bulletin, 1964. – E. ROSSI, "La prospettiva nella pittura moderna," Il Veltro, 1964. – W.V. ANDERSEN, "Cézanne's Carnet violet-moiré," The Burlington Magazine, 1965. – A. CHAPPUIS, "Cézanne dessinateur: copies et illustrations," Gazette des Beaux-Arts, 1965. – M. WALDFOGEL, "Caillebotte, Vollard and Cézanne's Baigneurs au repos," Gazette des Beaux-Arts, 1965. – T. REFF, "Cézanne and Hercules," The Art Bulletin, 1966; "Pissarro's Portrait of Cézanne," The Burlington Magazine, 1967. – W.V. ANDERSEN, "Cézanne, Tanguy, Chocquet," The Art Bulletin, 1967. – H. PERRUCHOT, "Cézanne," Le Jardin des Arts, 1967. – M. SCHAPIRO, "The Apples of Cézanne," Art News Annual, 1968. – J. REWALD, "Chocquet et Cézanne," Gazette des Beaux-Arts, 1969. – M.

DELLIS, "Notes relatives à quelques dessins de Paul Cézanne conservés au Cabinet des Estampes du Musée de Bâle," Gazette des Beaux-Arts, 1971. – M. HOURS, "Cézanne's Portrait of his Father," History of Art, National Gallery of Art, Washington 1971–1972. – J. REWALD, "Cézanne and his Father," History of Art, National Gallery of Art, Washington 1971–1972. – D.W. DRUICK, "Cézanne, Vollard and Lithography: The Ottawa Maquette for the Large Bathers Colour Lithograph," Bulletin of the National Gallery of Canada, Ottawa 1972. – M. TOSHIKUNI, "Les débuts de l'impressionnisme chez Cézanne," Information d'Histoire de l'Art, 1974. – U. PERUCCHI-PETRI, "War Cézanne Impressionist? Die Begegnung zwischen Cézanne und Pissarro," Du, 1975. – J. REWALD, "Some entries for a new catalogue raisonné of Cézanne's paintings," Gazette des Beaux-Arts, 1975.

Special Issues of Periodicals

Mercure de France, 1 August 1905. – L'Amour de l'Art, December 1920 (M. DENIS, E. FAURE, J. GASQUET, E. JALOUX, S. LÉVY). – L'Amour de l'Art, January 1921 (C. CAMOIN, W. GEORGE, M. LAFARGUE). – L'Amour de l'Art, May 1936 (R. HUYGHE and J. REWALD). – La Renaissance, May-June 1936 (P. JAMOT, J. COMBE, C. STERLING, J. VERGNET-RUIZ, C. TOLNAY). – L'Art Sacré, May 1936 (M. DENIS, J. REWALD, H. HÉRAUT). – Le Point, August 1936 (Cézanne et la Provence by J. REWALD and L. MARSCHUTZ).

Exhibitions

Group exhibitions of the Impressionists, Paris 1874, 1877. – Salon des XX, Brussels 1890. – Exposition Décennale, Paris 1890. – Galerie Vollard, Paris 1895, 1898, 1899. – Salon des Indépendants, Paris 1899, 1901, 1902, 1905. – Centennale de l'Art français, Paris 1900. – Salon de la Libre Esthétique, Brussels 1901, 1904. – Salon d'Automne, Paris 1904, 1905, 1906, 1907. – Galerie Bernheim-Jeune, Paris 1907, 1910, 1914, 1920, 1922, 1924, 1926, 1935, 1939. – Musée de l'Orangerie, Paris 1936 (catalogue: J.E. BLANCHE, P. JAMOT, C. STERLING). – Centenaire de Paul Cézanne, Musée des Beaux-Arts, Lyons 1939 (catalogue: J. BILLIET). – Centenaire du peintre indépendant Paul Cézanne, Société des artistes indépendants, Paris 1939 (catalogue: M. DENIS). – Art Institute of Chicago and Metropolitan Museum of Art, New York 1952 (catalogue: D. CATTON RICH and T. ROUSSEAU). – Monticelli et le baroque provençal (23 Cézannes), Musée de l'Orangerie, Paris 1953 (catalogue: G. BAZIN). – Museums of Aix-en-Provence, Nice and Grenoble 1953 (catalogue: J. LEYMARIE). – Hommage à Cézanne, Paris 1954 (catalogue: A. CHATELET). – Edinburgh Festival and Tate Gallery, London 1954 (catalogue: L. GOWING). – Le cinquantenaire de la mort de Cézanne, Pavillon de Vendôme, Aix-en-Provence 1956. – Kunsthaus, Zürich 1956 (catalogue: G. JEDLICKA). – Gustave Geffroy et l'art moderne, Paris 1957 (catalogue: J. VALLÉRY-RADOT). – Catalogue des peintures, pastels, sculptures impressionnistes du musée du Louvre by H. ADHÉMAR, Paris 1958. – Paul Cézanne 1839–1906, Österreichische Galerie im Oberen Belvedere, Vienna 1961. – Cézanne, Gauguin, Van Gogh, Seurat. Wegbereiter der modernen Malerei, Kunstverein, Hamburg 1963. – Le Paysage français de Cézanne à nos jours, Museum Boymans-van Beuningen, Rotterdam 1963. – Cézanne Watercolors, Knoedler Galleries, New York 1963 (catalogue: M. SCHAPIRO, R. WITTKOWER, T. REFF). – La collection Jean Walter-Paul Guillaume, Paris 1966 (catalogue: M.T. LEMOYNE DE FORGES). – Cézanne Watercolors, Pasadena Art Museum, California 1967 (catalogue: J. COPLANS). – Cézanne. An Exhibition in Honor of the Fiftieth Anniversary of the Phillips Collection, Washington, Chicago, Boston 1971. – Catalogue du musée du Jeu de Paume by A. DAYEZ, Paris 1973. – Watercolour and Pencil Drawings by Cézanne, London 1973 (catalogue: L. GOWING and R. RATCLIFFE). – Cézanne dans les musées nationaux, Paris 1974 (catalogue: H. ADHÉMAR, M. HOOG, G. MONNIER). – Le Centenaire de l'Impressionnisme, Paris 1974 (catalogue: A.M. CLARK, A. DAYEZ, M. HOOG, C. MOFFETT). – Cézanne, Tokyo 1974 (catalogue: J. REWALD, D. SUTTON, F. NOVOTNY, A. CHAPPUIS, C. IKEGAMI). – Cézanne, The Late Work, Museum of Modern Art, New York, and Museum of Fine Arts, Houston 1977 (catalogue: T. REFF, L. GOWING, L. BRION-GUERRY, J. REWALD, F. NOVOTNY, G. MONNIER, D. DRUICK, G.H. HAMILTON, W. RUBIN); and Grand Palais, Paris 1978 (catalogue: H. ADHÉMAR, L. BRION-GUERRY, A. CHAPPUIS, G. MONNIER, J. REWALD, W. RUBIN).

List of Illustrations

Figures preceded by the letter V. refer to the catalogue raisonné compiled by Lionello Venturi: *Cézanne, son art, son œuvre*, 2 volumes, Paul Rosenberg, Paris 1936.

Figures preceded by the letter C. refer to the catalogue compiled by Adrien Chappuis: *The Drawings of Paul Cézanne, A Catalogue Raisonné*, 2 volumes, New York Graphic Society, Greenwich, Connecticut, 1973.

Works listed without photographic credit are reproduced from photographs belonging to the estate of Lionello Venturi.

171

PAUL CÉZANNE: DRAWINGS AND ETCHINGS

OTHER ARTISTS

PHOTOGRAPHS

Index of Names and Places

PUBLISHED AUGUST 1978
PICTURE EDITOR: LAURO VENTURI
PRINTED BY
ROTO-SADAG S.A., GENEVA

Printed in Switzerland